"*...loaded with maps, photos and detailed descriptions.*"   – **Marin Independent Journal**

"*...not only offers clear directions for hikers of moderate abilities; it is also a guide to unrevealed places where a little exertion and an adventurous spirit can make the wild beauties of Point Reyes come alive for you.*"
  –**San Francisco Chronicle/***Outdoors section*

"*...a must for those who wish to find a magic kingdom.*"   –**The San Mateo Times**

POINT REYES
Secret Places and Magic Moments

by Phil Arnot

WIDE WORLD PUBLISHING/TETRA

Point Reyes–Secret Places & Magic Moments

Published by
Wide World Publishing/Tetra
P.O. Box 476
San Carlos, CA 94070, USA
telephone: (415) 593-2839

photographs by Phil Arnot

cover: Wildcat Beach, Point Reyes National Seashore

Revised Edition 1988

My introduction to the land that was to become Point Reyes National Seashore was in 1933. My grandmother knew some people who lived in Bear Valley and because of her infectious charm and enthusiasm for nature, she was given virtual carte blanche to this then remote ranch country. Tagging along with her on one of her visits I got to see and appreciate something of this area as early as age nine. I remember bay trees arching over the Bear Valley road, the tall firs bearded with Spanish moss, and the sound of Bear Valley Creek gurgling under the thick bushes along the road. Little did I know that I would someday come to explore the whole area until I knew intimately the high hills overlooking the sea, the deep forests, the perenially green meadows, the sandy beaches, the steep cliffs rising abruptly off the beach, the waterfalls plunging into the sea, the wildlife, the ocean caves and the springtime wind that sets the hillside grasses and flowers to dancing.

Point Reyes National Seashore
South District Map

Sir Francis Drake Hwy.

Pt. Reyes Station

CONTINUED ON NEXT MAP

Bayview Trail 2.3

Limantour Road

Bayview Trail 0.7

Laguna Trail

Sky Trail 0.7

Estero Trail

Muddy Hollow Trail 1.4

Limantour Trail 0.2

Hostel 0.3

Education Center 1.8

Fire Lane Trail 2.2

Coast Trail 0.4

Laguna Trail 0.6

Limantour

Coast Trail 2.8

Sky Camp 1.0

Horse Trail

Mt. Wittenberg 1407

Bear Valley Road

miles

Fire Lane Trail 1.0

Coast Camp 1.3

Sky Trail 1.4

Olema

Sir Francis Drake

0.7 Sky Trail

Meadow Trail 1.5

Bear Valley

1.3

Woodward Valley Trail 1.8

0.3

Old Pine Trail 1.9

Bear Valley Trail 0.8

Rift Zone Trail

PACIFIC OCEAN

Coast Trail 2.3

Baldy Trail 1.4

Divide Meadow

Private Property

GOLDEN GATE NATIONAL RECREATION AREA

1.6

Bolinas Ridge Trail

Kelham Beach

Sky Trail 1.2

Baldy Trail 1.0

4.9

Arch Rock

Bear Valley Trail 0.5

Greenpicker Trail 1.5

4.3

0.7

Coast Trail 1.4

0.8

2.1

REMEMBER!

No Firearms
Carry Water
No Wood Fires
Hazardous Cliffs
Beware of Tides
Help Prevent Erosion—Do Not Short Cut Trails
Camping by Permit Only
No Dogs on Trails
Dial Emergency 911

Glen Camp Loop 0.9

Glen Camp 1324

Fivebrooks

1.2

0.8

0.9

Bear Valley Trail 0.7

Bolinas Trail 1.1

Wildcat Camp

Wildcat Lake

Mud Lake 0.8

1.3

Ocean Lake

Stewart Trail 3.3

TRAILHEAD DISTANCES

BEAR VALLEY TO: Miles

Sky Camp	2.7
Arch Rock	4.1
Glen Camp	4.6
Wildcat Camp	6.3
Coast Camp	8.9
Palomarin	11.8

PALOMARIN TO:

Bass Lake	2.6
Pablo Point	4.0
Double Point	4.0
Wildcat Camp	5.5
Glen Camp	8.0
Coast Camp	13.2

FIVEBROOKS TO:

Bear Valley	4.4
Glen Camp	5.0
Wildcat Camp	5.7
Palomarin	7.7

LIMANTOUR TO:

Coast Camp	2.3
Sky Camp	5.9
Arch Rock	6.5

Alamere Falls

Crystal Lake

Lake Ranch Trail 2.5

Olema Valley Trail

Double Point

Pelican Lake

Bass Lake

0.6

0.9

Crystal Lake Trail

2.3

2.3

0.7

Teixeira Tr. 1.1

2.2

Coast Trail

Ridge Trail 1.0

Pablo Point

Ridge Trail 2.3

Palomarin

Point Reyes Bird Observatory

Mesa Rd.

📞	Phone
🐴	Stables
🏕	Picnic Area
🚶	Trailhead Parking
🏛	Park Headquarters
⛺	Backcountry Campground

- – – – – Trails
- +++++ Unmaintained Trails
- ——— Roads / Highways
- ▬▬▬ Park Boundary
- •••••••• Bicycle Trails

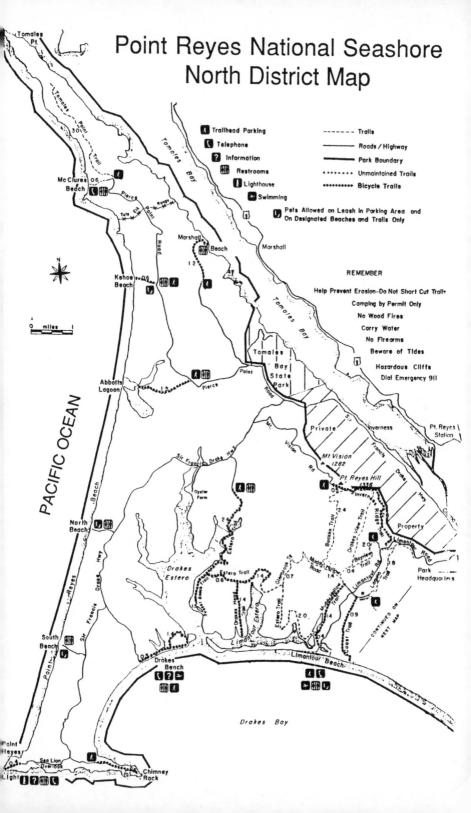

Point Reyes National Seashore
North District Map

Legend:

- 🅿 Trailhead Parking
- ☏ Telephone
- ? Information
- 🚻 Restrooms
- 🗼 Lighthouse
- 🏊 Swimming
- 🐾 Pets Allowed on Leash in Parking Area and On Designated Beaches and Trails Only

- ------ Trails
- ——— Roads / Highway
- ━━━━ Park Boundary
- +++++ Unmaintained Trails
- •••••• Bicycle Trails

REMEMBER

Help Prevent Erosion-Do Not Short Cut Trails

Camping by Permit Only

No Wood Fires

Carry Water

No Firearms

Beware of Tides

Hazardous Cliffs

Dial Emergency 911

Tomales Pt.

Tomales Point Trail 3.0

McClures Beach 0.6

Pierce Point Road

Tule Elk

Kehoe Beach 0.6

Marshall Beach 1.2

Marshall

Abbotts Lagoon

Pierce 1.5

Tomales Point

Tomales Bay

Tomales Bay State Park

Private

Inverness

Pt. Reyes Station

PACIFIC OCEAN

North Beach

Abbotts Lagoon

Sir Francis Drake Hwy.

Oyster Farm

Estero Trail 2.0

Mt. Vision Rd.

Mt Vision 1282

Pt. Reyes Hill 1316

Inverness Ridge Trail

Bucklin Trail 2.4

Drakes View Trail

Sir Francis Drake Hwy.

Property

Limantour Road

Park Headquarters

Point Reyes Beach

Drakes Estero

Estero Trail 0.6

Estero Trail 1.4

Glenbrook

Estero Trail 2.0

Muddy Hollow Road

Bayview Trail 0.4

Limantour Rd.

Coast Trail 0.9

CONTINUED ON NEXT MAP

South Beach

Drakes Beach

Limantour Beach

Drakes Bay

Point Reyes

Sea Lion Overlook

Light

Chimney Rock

0 miles 1

TO THE READER

The descriptions in this book have to do with geographic locations of unusual natural and/or aesthetic character. To reach these locations one must proceed on foot, often over untrailed terrain, including coastlines. There is some inherent personal risk involved in the undertakings thus described in this book as there always is whenever one ventures forth to hike and explore the natural world. It should be added that some of the hikes described herein are not for inexperienced hikers, but all hikers, whatever their level of competence, should be cautious and attentive especially when off trail, on narrow beaches and near rocky headlands. No wilderness leader, no book on wilderness exploration can do more than warn and caution where specific known dangers exist. However, in the wilderness, as in life, there is always the unexpected. And even when the forewarned are properly cautious and attentive to known dangers, accidents sometimes happen. Whenever I undertake a wilderness outing I accept the risks entirely on my own responsibility. I expect that my readers will do no less when seeking the secret places and magic moments at Point Reyes National Seashore or anywhere else.

Phil Arnot

———INTRODUCTION ———

15   Point Reyes National Seashore as Wilderness

———SECRET PLACES ———

23   Miller Cave
31   Elephant Cave
41   Real Secret Beach
47   Sculptured Beach
59   Double Point Cove Overlook
65   Wild Huckleberries
71   Phantom Falls
79   Secret Cave & Secret Beach
89   The Unknown Coast
99   A Dogwood & A Dawn Redwood

SECRET PLACES &
——— MAGIC MOMENTS ———

105   WIldcat Beach Overlook
111   Alamere Falls
117   Tomales Point
125   Drama at Elephant Rock

———MAGIC MOMENTS ———

131   Alone in the Wilderness
139   Panoramic Hill
145   Wildcat Beach & Camp
153   Whale Watching
163   A Walk in the Piny Woods
169   Bear Valley by Moonlight
175   Kehoe Beach in May
181   The Sea Tunnel in a storm
187   Moonrise at Drakes Beach
193   Mount Wittenberg
199   McClures Beach

To the memory of Fred "Fritz" Berensmeier

View down northern Wildcat Beach toward Double Point

Point Reyes
National Seashore
– as Wilderness

*"Every day was a holiday and
all the world lay before me."*
– John Muir

Sunset at McClures Beach

Much of the publicity surrounding Point Reyes National Seashore since its creation 25 years ago has given that region a semi-tourist aura. The existence of some paved roads cutting through the National Seashore, a Visitor Center within the park, and the proximity of a few hotels, restaurants, and bed and breakfast establishments have helped, no doubt, create Point Reyes National Seashore in the image of a kind of maritime Muir Woods. Articles in newspapers and magazines have, over the years, characterized Point Reyes as a mecca for sightseers who need only to drive their cars from one "point of interest" to another. Less extreme publicity has been more balanced in its portrayal, yet the image of Point Reyes National Seashore as a kind of amalgamation of Muir Woods and Marine World persists. "I hear you can practically drive right up to the sea lions" one urbanite commented to me not long ago. "Do they have a restaurant at Drakes Beach" (yes they do, and a good one) asked a woman in an audience right after I had shown a slide program extolling the wild aspects of Point Reyes. On any given weekend the Visitor Center has its share of citizens browsing among the books and excellent exhibits, Drakes Beach has its surfers, the lighthouse parking lot is full as whale watchers swarm the nearby hillsides and Limantour Beach has its volleyball games, frizbees, and leashed dogs. Even the runners, myself included, have discovered the up and down trails of the National Seashore. The self-guiding one mile Earthquake Trail, with its informative display boards attracts its share of visitors. And the reconstructed Miwok Village captures, as much as any reconstruction can, a sense of who was here first and who truly lived at Point Reyes. The very name, "Visitor Center", of the main facility at the Bear Valley Trailhead (Park Headquarters) is consistent with the image of Point Reyes National Seashore as a place where you look at exhibits, go on guided walks, and drive out to scenic vista points, and, generally, "visit" the region. All this is good and necessary, I suppose, but there is much more to Point Reyes than a "place of interest." Most of Point Reyes is wilderness, a natural region only slightly diminished in its natural state by human intervention. Therein lies, I believe, the primary value of Point Reyes National Seashore.

Only in a bona fide wilderness can one find the collection of different yet uniquely related experiences, all of them uplifting, some of them profound, that make up the totality of *the wilderness experience.* In the wilderness one experiences *Beauty* in all its varied manifestations – pure, simple, and timeless. One experiences *Silence* – so utter that it is heard and one feels its soothing penetration. One experiences *Humility* in the presence of nature's magnitude and, at the same time, one feels a sense of communion with one's surroundings. Even a sense of kinship. There is a sense of *Love* in the wilderness – of instinctively loving what one sees and hears and of being loved by all that surrounds. In the wilderness one experiences a sense of *Infinity* – even a vague sense that all that exists, however it may change, will always exist. All of this is not to say that the average person slips into some kind of mystic state the moment he or she leaves the parking lot. The wilderness experience, as a sum total of individual but related experiences, is usually subtle, even unconscious much of the time. Much of the time we are too involved in conversation, nature study, or some other cognitive activity to be consciously touched by our wild surroundings. Only when one is open and receptive does one feel the touch of wilderness. With time and patience, however, the receptive capacity and affinity grow. Then the communion between the individual and his/her surroundings becomes conscious and grows in intensity. The main point here is that, while Point Reyes

National Seashore has a legitimate attraction as an educational and tourist region, its chief value lies in the intrinsic experiences inherent in that region's wilderness character. Our species has lived 99.9% of its existence in nature, in an ecologically compatible relationship with nature. Therefore, there is probably an inherent psychic rapport between ourselves and the wilderness with which the veneer of technology has interfered. Technology bred urbanization, and urbanization has isolated us from the natural environment. I can't prove it, but I think as a species we *miss* wilderness desperately – even if most of us don't consciously know it.

Point Reyes is a more varied wilderness region than most that I have known. In a single 10 mile walk one may experience open meadows, high hills with sweeping panoramas of land and sea, deep forests, sandy beaches, ocean caves and cliffs, streams, lakes and waterfalls plunging over cliffs onto beaches below. At Point Reyes there are deer (3 kinds!), fox, bobcat, skunk, chipmunk, squirrels, Tule elk, and once again, mountain lion. There is a great variety of bird life including puffins, pelicans, cormorants, kites, marsh hawks, and red tailed hawks. From the hillsides one sometimes spots a whale. Along the beach one always sees in the afternoon three or more seals 30-100 yards off-shore. Occasionally a whale can be seen from the shoreline as well. Sea lions can be observed from above at Sea Lion Cove. Wild flowers abound in springtime – iris, paint brush, lupine, tidy-tips, buttercups, forget-me-nots, goldenrods, yarrow, monkey flower, filddleneck, milkmaids, blue bells, poppies, seaside daisies, goldenrod, and many more. Rain forest cover the high ridges and hill slopes at Point Reyes. Douglas fir predominates. Bishop pine, unique to the Point Reyes region, is prevalent in the northern portion of the park. Oak, madrone and California laurel (bay) are scattered amidst the firs. Coyote brush is the dominant shrub along with bush lupine and lilac, all growing in the open. Beneath the stately forests of the Inverness Ridge huckleberry, sword ferns, nettle, blackberry, and mugwart live in perennial shade.

When one has known all the varied, yet related experiences that make up the wilderness at Point Reyes one is impressed with the fact that such an environment exists less than 30 miles from downtown San Francisco. Considering that 25 years ago developers had their eye – and money – on the Point Reyes region and considering that we are a "progress" oriented society, the creation of Point Reyes National Seashore, a park of such size having such proximity to the Bay Area, is remarkable. One wonders who to thank of the heroes and heroines in the struggle to set the region aside as wilderness – individuals and organizations. Their success speaks not only of their own sensitivity, vision, and persistence. It reflects on the rest of us. In spite of our preoccupation with material things, in spite of consumerism, and our mad race to accomplish and succeed we, or enough of us, are still just enough in touch with wilderness as to constitute a constituency for those who fought for wilderness in the halls of Congress. If that being in touch springs from an innate affinity for what is wild, as I think it does, then there is still hope for ourselves and the world. I feel that hope when I witness the joy that comes to people – neophytes and old-timers alike – from a day in the gentle wilderness of Point Reyes National Seashore.

Real Secret Beach at Point Resistance at high tide

Looking seaward from within the southern arm of horseshoe shaped Miller Cave at very low tide

Miller Cave
A Secret Place

"A seldom seen secret place right under the noses of many hikers on the most populated section of the Point Reyes National Seashore interior..."

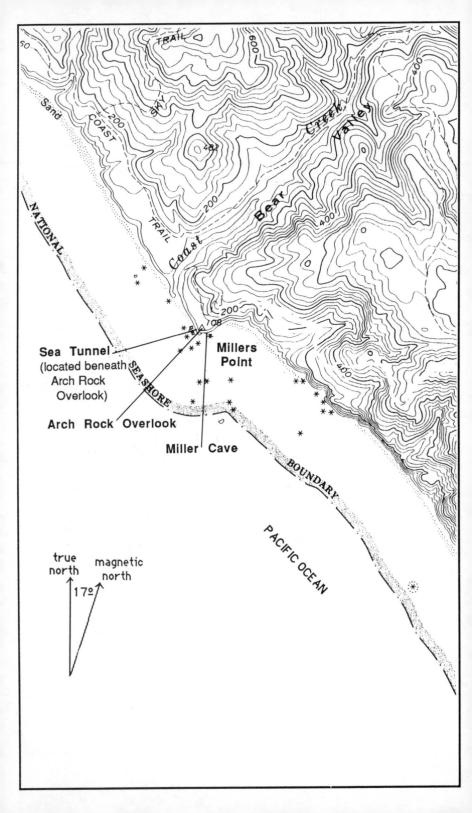

A seldom seen secret place right under the noses of many hikers on the most populated section of the Point Reyes National Seashore interior is *Miller Cave.* I call it the Miller Cave since it is part of the promontory that is Miller Point[1]. At Arch Rock Overlook at the very head of Bear Valley and right at the cliff edge of the Coast Creek there is a footpath leading to the shore of Coast Creek as it completes its 3 1/2 mile journey to Drakes Bay from Divide Meadow in Bear Valley. Coast Creek plunges through the sea tunnel (now two tunnels separated by a single rock pillar since the forces of erosion created the second tunnel in the early spring of 1986) and onto the sands directly below Arch Rock Overlook 30 feet above. Immediately south of the Sea Tunnel (8 feet long) is a small beach which can be looked down upon from Arch Rock Overlook. The beach in question can only be reached by crossing Coast Creek. This necessitates leaving the footpath connecting Arch Rock Overlook with the Sea Tunnel, a trail only 50-70 yards long, and either fording the creek near the mouth of the Sea Tunnel or hopping rocks across the creek preliminary to doing a short but exposed cliff traverse. Hundreds of people manage to gain access to the small beach in question by either route every weekend, but there is some risk and caution should be exercised. I have probably done the rock traverse 100 times in the last 27 years, but I am always mindful that over confidence and my first mistake might leave me severely injured. **So proceed with caution and at your own risk.**

Once on the small beach (100 yards long) walk southward away from Arch Rock Overlook and the Sea Tunnel. Immediately you'll observe some gently sloping and relatively smooth slab rock. Traverse the rocks at a slightly (5º-10º) upward angle for about 50-60

---

[1] Do not attempt to pass through at any tide higher than minus 0.1. Choppy seas can even complicate this condition and make passage inadvisable.

feet and you'll come upon a cliff edge that overlooks an inundated cave (at high and medium tides). The sea is 20-25 feet below as it fills the cave with slapping and churning water. From the vantage point one can look into the cave for some distance but not far enough to see that the cave is a kind of horseshoe which

Keyhole leading to Miller Cave as seen from the south.

turns in and out around a massive pillar of rock. At very low tides one can enter Miller Cave from the kelp covered rocky shoreline contiguous with the sandy beach already described. Going into the cave, which has enough light coming into it to enable you to see what you're doing, from the aforementioned beach is tricky. The rocks are wet. Some are covered with kelp so you may have to resign yourself to wading. Twenty feet into the cave, from the north or Arch Rock approach, one encounters, even at extremely low tides, an inky greenish-black pool of deep water. Passage will be to the left of the pool with the north wall of the cave to your left. Using somewhat damp hand and footholds on the north wall of the cave one can gingerly pass the pool in a 6-8 foot stretch that requires attention (advisable to do this section without your day pack which can be relayed across to whoever has gone first). Past the pool, which is about 7-8 feet long, you'll find yourself in the dimly but adequately lit interior of the cave. The ceiling begins to slant downward at this point so that the cave ends some 20-30 feet past the pool. The ceiling may still be dripping from the high tides of a few hours earlier or, in spring, seeping ground water from the land mass above the cave. From the cave's interior the continuing route is obvious. Pass the massive pillar which makes of the cave a kind of horseshoe and, in doing so, turn back along the cave's south wall towards the sea. In most low tide situations there will be some generally tranquil water in the cave so that you may need to wade in ankle or knee deep water. Or you can keep to the edge of the south wall and step along the wet rock at the base of the south wall towards a gently sloping rock face some 30-40 feet from the cave's interior. Climb the easy face of the rock face (10°-15°) to a point about 10 feet above the cave. As you climb you will be turning left, or southeastward, leaving your back to the cave. Almost immediately upon ascending 10 feet on the gently sloping rock face you'll have your first view of Wildcat Beach. All that is left, if you wish to go on to Wildcat Beach and points beyond, is to do a descending traverse of a solid rock wall which is less than sheer and is some 10-12 feet above the water at the highest point. Having made the descending traverse (60-70 feet in distance), you'll find yourself faced with a boulder hop over rocks some of which will be slippery with slimy kelp. *So exercise caution.* 100 yards of boulder hopping (6"-15" boulders) will put you on the sands of Wildcat Beach. From your first contact with the beach it is slightly over a mile to Wildcat Camp and some 100 yards to a seasonal waterfall which, in spring, gushes over a 12 foot cliff onto the beach. Still farther down the beach towards Wildcat Camp is *Phantom Falls* .

Miller Cave should never be attempted except at minus low tides so check the tide tables or call Park Headquarters ahead of time for their tide information. Stronger or better coordinated hikers should be prepared to help those who are not so strong or coordinated. If there is cooperation within the party, there should be no problems.

Transversing rock wall inside the southern arm of the horseshoe shaped Miller Cave.

Northward view from the edge of Miller Cave–Arch Rock Overlook in background.

Looking into Elephant Cave toward the eastern entrance as taken from the western entrance during low tide

Elephant Cave
A Secret Place

"Situated along a narrow rocky beach contained by high and crumbly cliffs, the cave is very difficult to reach."

This adventure should only be undertaken at **minus low tide conditions** and when careful observation of the route reveals that one may proceed safely.

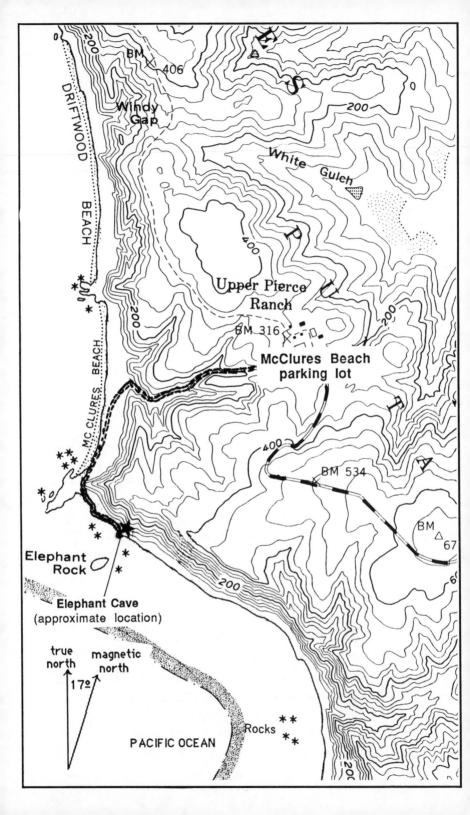

B y far the largest cave – almost a cavern – Elephant Cave is situated on the extreme northern coastline of Point Reyes National Seashore on the wild beach opposite Elephant Rock. I call it *Elephant Cave* because Elephant Rock, 100 yards off-shore, looks as though it would just fit inside.

Situated along a narrow rocky beach contained by high and crumbly cliffs , the cave is very difficult to reach. It is not shown on any of the USGS 15 minute or 7.5 minute topo maps, the Ericsson Map, the Park Service handout map, or Dee Molenaar's Pictorial Landform Map.

Elephant Cave is about 150 feet long from one entrance to the other. It is about 30 feet high at the western entrance while the ceiling at dead center is about 10-12 feet. The arched ceiling, which lowers as one moves from the western to eastern opening, is of granite rock, uneven and occasionally fractured. In exiting or entering at the narrower eastern end one needs to stoop only slightly, though it is remotely possible that an unusual high tide occurring during a storm could result in partial and temporary (another high tide storm could rearrange and reopen the entrance) plugging. On the south flank of the cave is a large alcove with two tunnels channeling in two different directions to the sea about 20-30 feet beyond dead center in the alcove. Most of the floor of the cave consists of loose rock rolled smooth by centuries of tidal action and resting on a sandy underflooring. However, the western entrance of the cave has a sandy floor though two or three steps seaward one finds smooth and deeply embedded granite rocks. The composition of the cave flooring will, no doubt, change slightly from season to season as high tide storms excavate and erode.

Mc Clures Beach –view southward during unusually high tide.

Elephant Cave is the scene of dramatic action at high tide, but one should witness this only from the eastern entrance which is situated some 15-20 feet above the beach. However, one would have to remain in this location until the tide turned sufficiently as to permit a return along the narrow beach by which one approached the cave a few hours earlier at low tide. In other words, the high tide one came to witness in the cave would, if high enough, cut off a retreat. *Low tide is the best and safest time for exploring the cave.*

There is only one safe route to Elephant Cave. This involves driving on the Pierce Road, from Olema and Inverness, to McClures Beach parking lot and walking down to McClures Beach (.6 mile). Once on the beach, turn southwestward towards the massive rock seen at the far end of the beach some 400 to 500 yards away. As you approach the rock, which jets out into the sea, notice a small notch between it and the rocky headland immediately to the left of the notch. Pass through the notch onto the small beach beyond - a beach which I'll call the First Beach.

At the southern end of the First Beach is a truncated protrusion of solid rock. Traverse/climb the rock about 2 to 4 feet above the beach and the off-shore low tide water. Descend, then, 2 to 4 feet into the tide pools now visible on the other side of the rocky protrusion just climbed. Wade, cautiously, for 15 to 30 yards (depending on the tide and surf) through tide pools to a boulder field and, then, onto a small rocky beach beneath sheer cliffs. Some 70 yards beyond the aforementioned tide pools you will be surprised to come upon the mouth of a huge cave - Elephant Cave. The cave is actually a grass covered promontory, with a tunnel reaching deep into the promontory itself towards the headwall of cliffs running along the coastline. At its entrance

Elephant Cave is about 30 feet high. It extends some 130-150 feet inward with the ceiling gradually lowering and dripping constantly. At the eastern end of the cave is an opening some 4 feet high. However, as suggested earlier, it could be closed or blocked with rock, sand and driftwood. Should this condition exist, due to the combination of very high tides and very high seas, turn around and abandon the hike until a later date. There is no safe way around the shoreline from the front of Elephant Cave southward.

Assuming that the eastern end of Elephant Cave is open, as will most likely be the case, proceed through the tunnel to the opening. It consists of a hole at the point where the hollow promontory that is Elephant Cave meets the north-south running cliffs of the Unknown Coast. Having passed through the eastern opening of the cave you will find yourself looking down the exterior wall of the cave much as though you were perched on the sill of a huge open window. A small alcove beach lies some 20 feet, below your window sill. Should you wish to descend to the beach[1], it will probably be best to face in and carefully climb down the 65-75 degree rock face. The rock is fairly solid, something which cannot be said for most of the cliffs at Point Reyes.

It needs to be said that should one elect to explore father south, one may come upon a cliff over which hangs a weathered rope. The rope, which was probably placed by abalone fishermen, hangs from a metal stake.[2] I recommend that you do not attempt

---

[1] Bear in mind that the tide will turn sufficiently to cut off return to McClures Beach in about 30-40 minutes after the peak of the low tide.

[2] In a number of other locations—3 known to the author—similar ropes, probably placed by abalone fishermen, hang over steep cliffs.

to use the rope to ascend the cliff in as much as 1) the rope is very weathered and 2) the cliff consists of crumbly and loose rock. Further, an ascent using the rope requires depending entirely on the strength of a frayed rope, the attachment of the rope to the stake, and the security of the stake for safety. And *safety*   here would well mean one's life.

In our first edition of this book, I did present the rope as a possible descent and/or ascent mechanism for gaining access to Elephant Rock. However, examination of the rope and cliff, conversation with Park authorities, who are not responsible in any way for placement or maintenance of the rope,[3] and recognition that 99% of the hikers have probably never had rock climbing experience, much less practice in hauling themselves hand over hand up a cliff, causes me to strongly urge the reader to *avoid using any rope hanging over a cliff here or anywhere at Point Reyes National Seashore.*

Should the intrepid hiker find that his/her sense of adventure has been barely whetted by the exploration of Elephant Cave and, thus, be tempted by any dangling rope I suggest an alternative: south of Elephant Rock for 3 miles lies the Unknown Coast, a wild, unvisited stretch of beach with 100' plus seasonal waterfalls (winter/spring), unusual rock formations, intriguing tidepools, and 2 "keyholes" requiring some skill in pathfinding. Since exploring the Unknown Coast requires the same low tide required for exploring Elephant Cave one might as well consider continuing on to Kehoe Beach from Elephant Cave.

---

[3] The National Park Service at Point Reyes National Seashore intends to remove the existing rope, but it is my guess that, if it does, abalone fishermen will replace it with a new one which, in time, will become weathered. As a former rock climber, I would be very reluctant to trust a rope laid down by someone totally anonymous.

*First, however, see the chapter on the Unknown Coast, bearing in mind that this route is **only for very experienced hikers.*** The Unknown Coast provides a short adventure filled with the excitement of discovery and experience of wild beauty in a place few people ever see. It is an adventure in any season of the year though the two waterfalls will be active in the spring.

Eastern entrance to Elephant Cave as seen from the rocky beach described.

Real Secret Beach (center left at middle tide) as seen from above at Point Resistance (southern view) – Kelham Beach in background

Real Secret Beach–
A Secret Place

*"...whatever the history of the place name,
Secret Beach , that name should rightfully
apply to the small, hidden, and usually
inaccessible beach inside Point Resistance."*

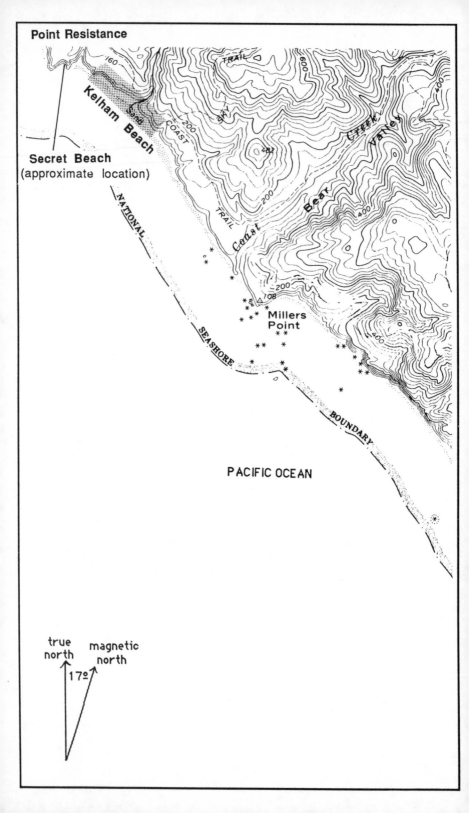

I n the early 1960's when Point Reyes National Seashore was in its infancy, I came across a unique cave and beach while exploring the coast one spring afternoon. Later I inquired at Park Headquarters as to whether or not the cave and beach had a name. At that time only one ranger knew of the existence of this location and she said that she thought the ranchers in the pre-park days called it *Secret Beach*. So that was the place name I always used when referring to this particular location at the north end of Kelham Beach. Then, in the mid 70's I saw the location named Secret Beach on a map designating the stretch of shoreline between Sculptured Beach and Point Resistance. Today this is the designation used in the USGS Point Reyes map. However, it seems to me that whatever the history of the place name, Secret Beach, that name should rightfully apply to the small, hidden, and usually inaccessible beach inside Point Resistance. The official Secret Beach may be inaccessible but it is not secret. But I'll let you decide for yourself.

To find what I will call *Real Secret Beach* take the Bear Valley Trail from the Visitor Center to Kelham Beach or come down from the Limantour Beach parking lot on the Coast Trail. In both cases some 5 miles are involved. At the junction of the Coast Trail and the Kelham Beach access trail, marked by an enormous Eucalyptus tree, proceed to Kelham Beach, walk to the water's edge, and turn right so as to face northwest towards the long arm of Point Resistance some 600 yards away. Notice that at a point on the arm of Point Resistance, which you would reach if you walked up those 600 yards of coastline, some terraced arches. These are your objective.

If the tide conditions permit (Check at the Visitor Center where an annual tide table is available at the desk. *A minus tide will be necessary for this exploration),* move up the beach toward the arches. 150 yards before reaching the arches, as you move up the beach, a small rock promontory jets out into the sea blocking, temporarily, the view of the arches. For one to safely continue the tide must must be sufficiently low as to enable one to walk around the promontory or, at worst, pass in between ankle deep waves. *If the waves are lashing the promontory do not continue. Always stop to study a questionable situation before moving on.*

Arches above cave leading to Secret Beach as described.

Once around the rock promontory proceed to the arches which, by now, will show themselves as the entrance to a large cave.

The cave is approximately 18 feet at the opening, 12 feet at the center, and 4 feet at the point where one passes through the far end and onto the Real Secret Beach. As you walk into the cave you'll notice, to your left, shallow surges of water coming in through a maze of small tunnels giving the sea access to the cave beneath the exterior walls of Point Resistance. The passage to the miniature beach has been, on very rare occasions, plugged up with sand. Trying to dig the opening free would probably be an exercise in futility. Better return in a few weeks when the sea will reopen the passage. The condition will change back to normal.

Real Secret Beach is a perfect 150 foot semi-circle. Scattered here and there on the beach, especially as one passes through the opening from the cave, are a number of large kelp covered boulders. Rising above the beach and extending in two protecting arms out into the sea beyond it are the near sheer cliffs of the interior of Point Resistance. Actually, Real Secret Beach is a small cove inside Point Resistance, accessible only through the aforementioned cave.

The cove can be seen from above if one breaks off the Coast Trail about 600 yards north of the giant Eucalyptus tree which stands on the junction of the Coast Trail and the Kelham Beach access trail. The route passes over an open and grassy plateau some 300 yards long to the cliffs above the open sea. Keep to the left of a large sea bird inhabited rock just offshore. The rock will become visible only in the last few yards as one approaches the edge of the cliffs. To find Real Secret Beach begin turning south about 100 yards from the western edge of the grassy plateau. Real Secret Beach inside the cove of Point Resistance will not be seen until you reach the edge of the appropriate cliff. 200 feet straight down is the cove and the beach at the east end.

Amphitheater

Sculptured Beach
A Secret Place

*"The adventure awaiting one at
Sculptured Beach does not require
expertise in rock climbing or sprinting."*

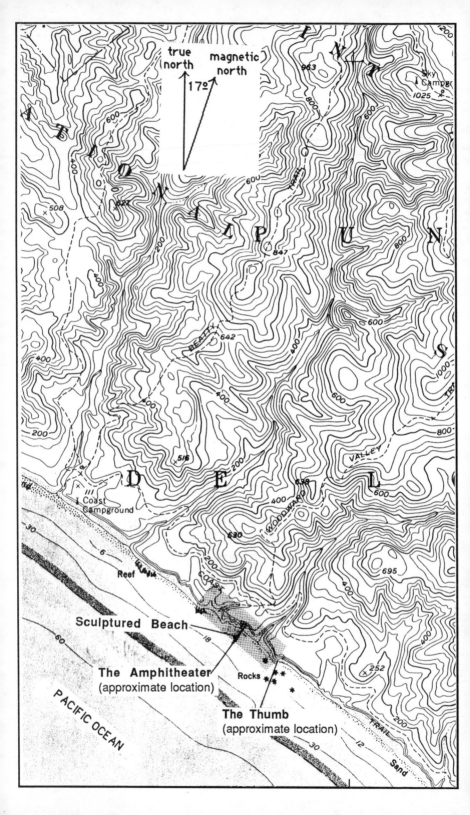

S *culptured Beach* is not far (2.5 miles) from a major trailhead[1] and, at low tide, it is readily accessible. It is close to a main trail, the Coast Trail, which is heavily traveled during summer months and on weekends throughout the rest of the year. Thus, one might expect to see large numbers of hikers and even sunbathers at Sculptured Beach. However, this is not the case. In 25 years of exploring and re-exploring Point Reyes National Seashore, I've seldom seen many people on the most accessible northern portion of Sculptured Beach and never more than two or three people on the less accessible southern section, which is often totally empty on the best of Saturdays or Sundays.

What makes Sculptured Beach worth exploring is, of course its sculpture – cliffs, amphitheaters, caves, and tunnels. Starting about 1/2 mile south of the Coast Camp and immediately south of a perennial unnamed creek (not to be confused with the Santa Maria Creek immediately north of Coast Camp and adjacent to the beach access trail connecting Coast Camp with the beach) one will observe the cliffs, sand colored and nearly sheer, that mark the beginning of Sculptured Beach. Some of the cliffs are fluted, others are dissected by narrow ravines cut by the seasonal flow of rainwater in spring. Wind and rain have carved and washed graceful lines on the soil composition of the cliff faces. Here and there, along the dark stains left by oozing subsurface water, yellow monkey flowers cling to the nearly 90º cliffs. Moving southward one comes upon a low arm of a solid but heavily eroded rock promontory which appears to block farther passage as one approaches it. However, after walking up natural steps to the top of the 3.5 - 4 foot promontory, one comes quickly upon its far edge (southern). At the edge , a mini cliff actually, one is

---

[1] Limantour Beach parking lot is a little over 2 miles of beach walking away from the northern portion of Sculptured Beach.

confronted with a 3-4 foot drop onto soft sand. The more confident hiker can easily jump it, though packs should be handed down to whoever goes first without a pack. Those who prefer may sit on the edge of the mini cliff and slide off onto the sand below.[2] Or the mini cliff can be descended by first facing in and then climbing down on the numerous hand and footholds. During minus low tides one can even walk around this intruding arm of granite rock, but beware of the slippery rocks at the water's edge.

Having gotten over the aforementioned obstacle, if it can be called an obstacle, one is now moving towards a much longer arm of protruding rocks some 200 yards ahead. Before reaching this next seeming obstacle one has the comfort of a narrow sandy beach which, just before the rock arm is encountered, turns inland to the base of the Sculptured Beach Access Trail coming down some 200 yards from the Coast Trail. This sheltered enclave is an excellent lunch, rest, or sunbathing spot inasmuch as it is generally protected from any wind which might be blowing.

To continue south to the ever less traveled sections of Sculp-tured Beach requires a low tide condition. The rock promontory containing the aforementioned sandy enclave cannot be passed by a shoreline route at the lowest of tides – the seaward cliffs are sheer to the water under any condition. Hence, one must pass over the rocky arm and on to the caves, coves, tunnels, and am-phitheaters just beyond – all requiring careful attention in their approach under the prerequisite low tide conditions. Careful ex-amination will reveal a natural staircase route leading to the top of the rock promontory at the base of a sharply

---

[2] Over the years this drop has changed from a 6-8 foot drop in the 60's and 70's to the 3.5-4 foot drop in the last 5 or 6 years. Over time the distance may become greater again as the sea continues to alter the beach.

sculptured knife-edge cliff protruding from the long line of cliffs paralleling the beach. At this point one is about 8 feet above the beach ahead (southward). Moving to the southern edge of the promontory, one can observe a narrow beach, directly below, flanked by yet another rock promontory barely 50 feet from the edge of the promontory on which one is now standing. The hiker/explorer will also observe a cave/tunnel, 11-12 feet high, 10 feet wide, and 4 feet long, offering a low tide passage to more secret places beyond. One will likewise observe, at the base of the north-south line of cliffs to the left, that there is a beach passage through a narrow corridor beyond which one cannot see from his/her present position. By this time the true adventurer is anxious to get down onto the beach, 8-10 feet below, and move on to see what mysteries are yet hidden from view by the promontory 50 feet away.

The next move requires descending to the elongated beach below by climbing down the rock. The rock is generally quite solid and offers plenty of good foot and hand holds. Cooperation – and especially patience – within a group will make the descent easier for those who are less experienced and/or less confident. One can do a traversing descent on the narrow ledges, just right for foot and handholds, leading towards the north/south cliffs to the left (east) or descend the rocky staircase facing the sea (the steps are long). Perhaps the easiest descent will be found at the base of the sand colored cliff to the left. Here a 4.5 foot jump onto the beach can be executed preferably from a sitting position at the edge of the rock promontory. Here, again, the assistance of others will make this safer and relatively easy.

Having surmounted the rock promontory behind, one is immediately faced with the next. However, since the adventure is being undertaken at low tide the intrepid hiker may either pass through the aforementioned cave/tunnel (slippery rocks), if the tide is low, or pass behind the rock promontory which is not quite connected

Along Sculptured Beach. Caves leading to Small Seal Beach.

to the north-south line of the cliff facing Drakes Bay. The latter passage is wide enough for two or three people to slip through walking abreast. It leads immediately to yet another miniature beach which I call *Small Seal Beach,* named because I once surprised a small seal sunning itself on the beach just as I turned through the narrow passage. Small Seal Beach is contained on the south by yet another rock promontory, 180 feet away, which has been hidden from view until one turns onto Small Seal

Beach. As one turns through the passage onto Small Seal Beach one passes a spring on the wall of the cliffs to the left. The spring is usually active year around though it never has more than a trickle of water except right after a period of heavy rains. Yellow monkey flowers cling tenaciously to the sheer walls of the cliff along the moistened path of the spring.

Once on Small Seal Beach and in sight of the next rock promontory which stretches an arm 100 feet or more into the sea, the hiker is fully aware why this adventure is being undertaken at low tide. Small Sea Beach extends less than 200 feet from the point where one slips through the narrow passage onto the beach to the next promontory. The beach is so narrow that at high tides the breakers wash up to the base of the cliffs.

The next, and last, move is obvious. But for a huge cave/tunnel close to the north/south running cliffs facing the sea the promontory would be a task for those skilled in rock climbing. During minus low tides one can walk through the cave/tunnel onto the next beach. At low tides which are not minus tides[3] one may have to race through the tunnel onto the next beach. Since the tunnel is roughly 12 feet high, 15 feet wide, and 3 feet long it is quickly and easily passed if the tide is barely reaching the inland wall. However, *if the breakers are reaching 2 or 3 feet on the wall the situation needs to be studied and tide tables consulted before proceeding. If the largest breakers are lashing at the opening to a height of 3 feet or more turn around or see if the low tide maximum is perhaps an hour or two away.* Sunbathing and/or lunch can occupy the time needed for the tide to recede sufficiently to

---

[3] At this writing the National Park Service is giving away tide tables appropriate to the calendar year.

allow easy passage through the cave/tunnel. If it is deemed safe to proceed the most able person should go first to test the route. It is safer to wear some kind of tennis type shoes or thongs because of hidden rocks. No more than two persons should go between breakers inasmuch as they might be too slow to enable two or three others, following behind, to turn the corner before the next wave. ***However, a person or party should not proceed if there is any danger that a wave could knock someone off his or her feet.*** When in doubt make a conservative decision and either turn back or wait for favorable tide conditions if the wait is of reasonable time. Beyond the last obstacle one has a broad sandy beach some 400 yards in length, to ex-

The seal that inspired the name Small Seal Beach.

plore. At the far end of this last section of Sculptured beach is a truncated rock promontory. Just off the shore from the promontory is a prominent rock pinnacle which I call *The Thumb* (mentioned in the chapter on Secret Beach). The Thumb divides Sculptured Beach from Secret Cave and Beach. Meanwhile, one very quickly passes what I call *The Amphitheater,* a perfect semi-circle of sandy beach cove set back into the wall of the sheer cliffs 100 feet above.The Amphitheater is sheltered from wind. It is a perfect spot for a siesta, lunch, sunbath or all three. 150 yards down the beach an unnamed creek cuts across the sands of another sandy section extending farther inland (eastward) than is the rule with the series of small beaches which make up Sculptured Beach. Piled up at the point where the creek pours out of a narrow wooded ravine onto the beach is a jumble of huge tree trunks and limbs, a log jam of mammoth driftwood thrown up by the severe high tide storms of winters past. One is impressed to see such huge limbs 10-15 feet up the ravine from the beach!

South of Sculptured Beach is Secret Beach, reached at low tide through what I call *the keyhole.* If the tide conditions permit one can cautiously extend the adventure to the intriguing features of that area. However, ***one needs to pay attention to the tide tables and to the actual behavior of the tide so that one can return to the northern portion of Sculptured Beach safely.*** *It takes about seven hours for most tides to go from maximum high to maximum low, but three hours after a given tide has reached its maximum low it may have turned sufficiently to block the return route in even less time than three hours.* ***So consulting tide tables isn't enough. One must keep an eye on what the tide is actually doing.***

The adventure awaiting one at Sculptured Beach does not require expertise in rock climbing or sprinting. I have led adult groups, including individuals in their 50's, 60's, and 70's through this area. Patience, cooperation, compassion, and good judgement will make the adventure a safe one and a joyful one. For many the experience is exhilarating.

Passing along Sculptured Beach toward the Thumb (in background) as described.

Along Sculptured Beach at low tide.

Double Point Cove as seen from Double Point Cove Overlook

Double Point Cove Overlook
A Secret Place

"...the National Park Service has closed Double Point Cove to hikers primarily to protect the seals and particularly the young pups. However, one can gain a magnificent overview of the entire cove, seals and all, from a cliff 350-400 feet above."

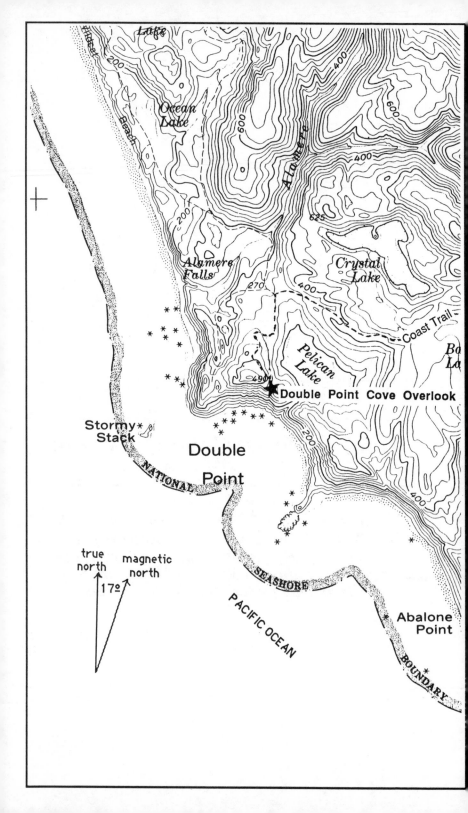

Double Point Cove, one of three major harbor seal rookeries in Point Reyes, is located in Point Reyes National Seashore between Palomarin Trailhead and Miller Point. The cove was well selected by the seals. Approach from the south is difficult because on the narrow beach between Palomarin Trailhead and the southern "point" of Double Point the waters of high and even medium tides press up against the base of the cliffs. From the north the approach is even more difficult. Coming down Wildcat Beach past Alamere Falls one finds the approach blocked by rocky cliffs which necessitate exposed rock climbing if one is to pass beyond to the cove. In addition to these natural obstacles, the National Park Service has closed Double Point Cove to hikers primarily to protect the seals and particularly the young pups. However, one can gain a magnificent overview of the entire cove, seals and all, from a cliff 350-400 feet above. With binoculars one can get an even better view of the seals than one could from inside the cove. I call this vantage point above the sea, *Double Point Cove Overlook.*

The harbor seals congregate on the beach towards the southern tip of Double Point when not swimming in the cove itself or in the sea at large. At first glance, particularly on a grey day, the mass of huddled seals appear as a collection of driftwood. But, as one watches, one or two will suddenly swim off the beach and into the water to remove any possible uncertainty for the viewer. Sometimes larger seals will position themselves on rock ledges which are part of the promontory which is the southern point of Double Point.

The shortest hiking approach to "Double Point Cove Overlook" is from Palomarin Trailhead about 3.5 miles south or, if one has come into Wildcat Camp on an overnight camping trip, by way of an easy day trip from the camp, roughly 1.5 miles of hiking to the overlook.

If coming from Palomarin Trailhead take the Coast Trail past Bass Lake, past the Crystal Lake Trail junction, and proceed downhill to a point where the Coast Trail levels off temporarily at a point some 200 yards from the north shore of Pelican Lake which is seen some 150 feet below. At this point head for the small saddle between 2 high hills to the southwest. The route to the saddle is through open brush covered terrain, mostly coyote brush, for approximately 300-350 yards. The gain in elevation is approximately 300 feet. One may find a faint foot path for much of the way to the saddle which is the Double Point Cove Overlook. Throughout this short ascent Pelican Lake is constantly in view to the left or southward.

If approaching the overlook from the North take the Coast Trail from Wildcat Camp and in approximately 1.5 miles of gently uphill walking, one reaches the departure point for Double Point Cove Overlook which is the temporary level spot in line with the saddle previously described.

Double Point along Wildcat Beach

On the Ridge Trail

Wild Huckleberries
A Secret Place

*"In most of these locations one can leave
the trail to squirm and wiggle through
thick underbrush to get berries most berry
pickers are not willing to work that hard for."*

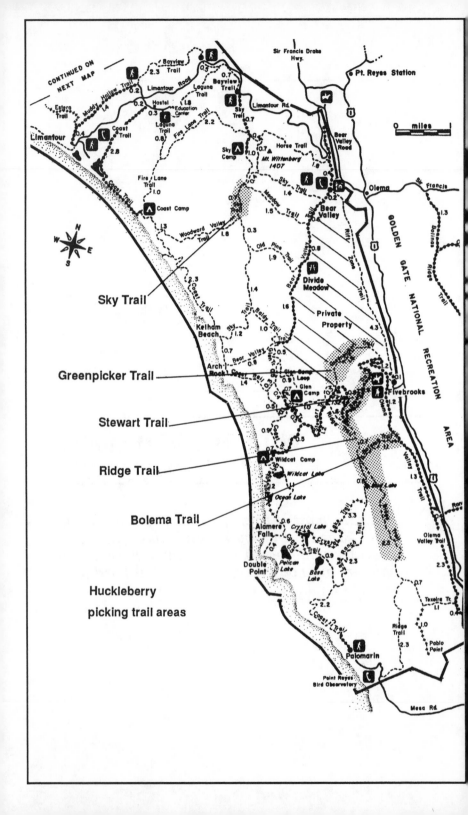

H uckleberries[1] grow wild and delicious in Point Reyes National Seashore! They are found on the heavily wooded ridges and slopes of the Inverness Ridge, the *spine* of the National Seashore, which runs through 60-65% of the park as it gradually declines before slipping under the sea at Tomales Point. The spring blossoms, white and delicate, turn to very dark blue or black berry in August and September. Huckleberries are delicious in muffins and pancakes or mixed with cereal.

The most abundant huckleberries are found, in season, on the Stewart Trail between Five Brooks and Fir Top, on the Greenpicker Trail between Five Brooks and Fir Top, on the Bolema Trail between Fives Brooks and the Ridge Trail, on the Ridge Trail for about 1-1.5 miles southward, on the Sky Trail between the Meadow Trail and the Woodward Valley Trail, along the Drake's view Trail after the first .7 mile out of the Bay View Trailhead, and off the Pierce Point Road between Sir Francis Drake Boulevard and the entrance to Tomales Bay State Park[2]. Take care to park your car completely off the road! In most of these locations one can leave the trail to squirm and wiggle through thick underbrush to get at berries most berry pickers are not willing to work that hard for.[3] If going off-trail be sure to keep your bearings. You'll lose sight of the trail as soon as you are 5-6 feet off of it. Take containers – one person can easily pick a gallon in a day – and a first aid kit with tweezers to deal with

---

[1] Evergreen Huckleberry (vacinium ovatum)

[2] In the case of the Greenpicker, Stewart, and Bolema Trails the huckleberries are not very prevalent until one has climbed two or three hundred vertical feet out of Five Brooks Trailhead.

[3] Wear long trousers, a full length shirt and/or coat, and gloves (when moving to a new picking spot). Blackberries, poison oak, and nettle will be encountered in all probability.

blackberry stickers which you may well brush into your hands as you become intent on reaching for that thick bunch of berries barely within arm's length. Those who are especially susceptible to poison oak should be well protected with long trousers and a long-sleeved shirt and, upon returning, wash with strong soap such as Fels-naptha.[4] Then sponge with rubbing alcohol. Wash the clothes also.

Certain west coast berries are poisonous. There isn't any poisonous berry which resembles a huckleberry at Point Reyes, but if you've never seen a huckleberry use a berry guide[5] and/or bring one to the Visitor Center for confirmation before eating or picking.

evergreen huckleberries

---

[4] Remember you can get poison oak by touching parts of your clothing which have had contact with poison oak and, then, touching your face or other parts of your body. Poison oak is a low shrub-like plant, bush or vine with shiny green leaves that turn red in the fall. Its main feature is that the leaves grow in clusters of three, with the central leaflet having a long stem. The leaflets resemble oak leaves.

[5] **Pacific Coast Berry Finder** by Glenn Keaton, PhD. Nature Study Guild 1978.

My grandmother knew where the huckleberries were in Marin County including the Point Reyes region. She'd go out at least once every autumn to spend the day picking enough to make huckleberry muffins and pancakes. Remembering how much I enjoyed what she served, I decided to include one of her recipes here.

Huckleberry Muffins

2 cups flour
3 1/2 teaspoons baking powder
1cup milk
3 tablespoons melted shortening
6 tablespoons sugar
1/2 teaspoon salt
1 egg, well beaten
3/4 cup berries

Combine sugar, egg and shortening. Sift flour. Measure and sift with salt and baking powder. Add alternately with milk to first mixture. Beat only until smooth. Fold in berries. Bake about 20 minutes at 400 degrees.

Phantom Falls during a dry season

Phantom Falls
A Secret Place

"As spectacular as Alamere Falls are there is another, equally spectacular and virtually unknown, waterfall farther up Wildcat Beach."

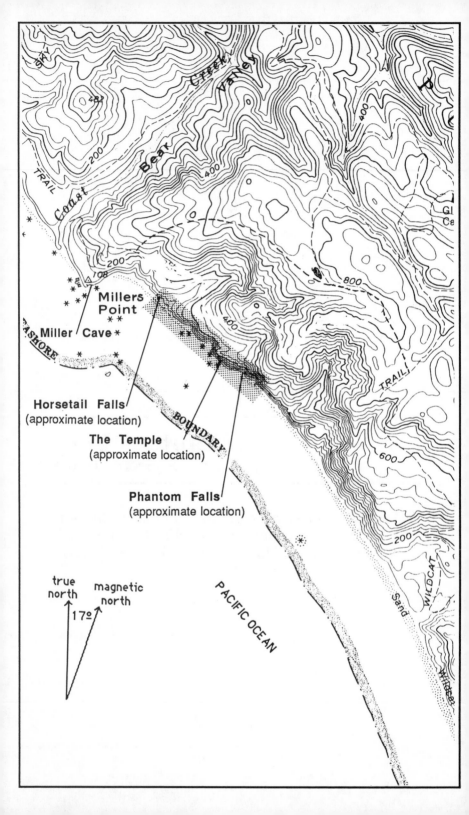

A nyone who has hiked appreciably in Point Reyes National Seashore knows of Alamere Falls situated about a mile south of Wildcat Camp on Wildcat Beach. The waters of Alamere Creek come gushing over the edge of the cliff some 30 feet above and then pour straight down to the sands of Wildcat beach in a display that is particularly impressive in spring. In fact, at this time of year the falls are almost as wide as they are high. At the highest of tides the falls plunge straight into the sea as it lashes against the cliffs at the base of the falls.

As spectacular as Alamere Falls are there is another, equally spectacular and virtually unknown, waterfall farther up Wildcat Beach. I call this fall, *Phantom Falls,* because it is seasonal and thus, active only for 2-4 months of the year depending on the amount of rainfall in a particular season. The source of Phantom Falls is not a major stream (it is not named on any map) such as Alamere Creek or Coast Creek which are perennial. Further, few people venture very far north on the beach beyond Wildcat Camp and, thus, do not know of Phantom Falls. And starting sometime between the end of April and Mid-May the falls will be dry. Hence there is nothing to see except, perhaps, the clusters of yellow monkey flowers growing on the moistened cliff along the course of the once active waterfall. However, in spring a steady stream of water comes bouncing off the nearly sheer cliff from the top of the falls some 150-200 feet above. It is, thus, the height of Phantom Falls, as well as its nearly sheer drop along a pathway of yellow monkey flowers, that makes it so spectacular.

If one takes a trip to Wildcat immediately after a heavy 2-3 day rainstorm the falls will be especially impressive. In contrast, the falls become a faintly audible trickle by late spring.

The Temple (looking northwestward)

To reach Phantom Falls come down the Bear Valley Trail from the Visitor Center and onto Wildcat Beach from the north through "Miller Cave" *only when the tide conditions permit (see Chapter on Miller Cave).* Since the approach through Miller Cave is seldom open, due to the fact that tides are usually too high to permit passage, three other less direct but more certain approaches should be considered: **(1)** Come up from Palomarin Trailhead out of Bolinas via the Coast Trail to Wildcat Camp (see **Exploring Point Reyes** by Phil Arnot and Elvira Monroe, Chapter 11). From Palomarin Trailhead to Wildcat Camp it is 5.4 miles. From the beach opposite Wildcat Camp to Phantom Falls, which are towards Miller Point and Arch Rock, it is slightly less than a mile. **(2)** Come in from Bear Valley Trailhead to Glen Trail (3.2 miles from the Visitor Center), go up the Glenn Trail for roughly 2 miles, cross over to the Coast Trail and follow it down to Wildcat Camp and Wildcat Beach some 2.5 miles from where you leave the Glen Trail for the Coast Trail. **(3)** Come in from the Visitor Center via the Bear Valley Trail all the way to the mouth of Bear Valley where the Bear Valley Trail junctions with the Coast Trail (4.0 miles). Turn left or southward on the Coast Trail, which crosses Coast Creek (foot bridge) and proceed over a scenic and circuitous route to Wildcat Camp and Wildcat Beach 3.5 miles from the junction of the Bear Valley Trail and the Coast Trail. **(4)** From on State Highway 1, Five Brooks Trailhead, which is 4 miles south of the Visitor Center follow either the Stewart Trail or Greenpicker Trail upward through the stately fir forest of the Olema Ridge to Fir Top (about 2 miles and 1140 vertical feet from Five Brooks Trailhead). From Fir Top follow the Stewart Trail downward and westward to its junction with the Coast Trail and continue on the Coast Trail to Wildcat Beach and Wildcat Camp (6.2 miles from Five Brooks Trailhead).

The Phantom Falls trip presents two other secret places worth mentioning. Between Miller Point and Phantom Falls is another unusual waterfall and a unique cave. These features have no official names, but I refer to them as *Horsetail Falls* and *The Temple.* When coming up the beach from Wildcat Camp, the temple is about 200 yards north of Phantom Falls and Horsetail Falls, which spouts out onto the sand from a truncated stream canyon 10 feet above the beach, is approximately 250 yards north of the Temple. I leave it to you to decide if my names for these features are appropriate.

To see Phantom Falls, and other unusual features nearby, on a day hike involves from 12 to 14 round trip miles depending on the route chosen. An alternative is to spend the night at Wildcat Camp (make reservations at the Visitor Center by phone well in advance – [415] 663-1092 – and take the 1 mile walk to Phantom Falls after pitching camp in the afternoon or the next morning–whenever the tide is favorable.

Horsetail Falls

Looking seaward from inside Secret Cave

The Secret Cave & Secret Beach
A Secret Place

"...an ocean cave the likes of which I have never seen before in 50 years of wilderness exploration. Few people know of its existence for it has no official name and is, thus, not identified on any map."

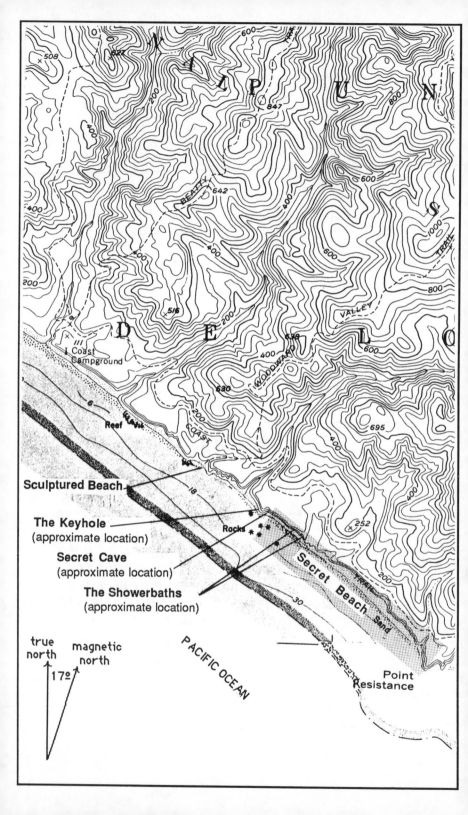

T here is, in the hinterland of Point Reyes National Seashore, an ocean cave the likes of which I have never
seen before in 50 years of wilderness exploration. Few
people know of its existence for it has no official name and is,
thus, not identified on any map. Nor is it shown or even suggested on any map by the configuration of contour lines. Further, it is
located on a stretch of inaccessible beach, *Secret Beach,* between Sculptured Beach and Point Resistance. I discovered the
cave for myself in 1962, the year the National Seashore was es-
tablished, during one of those rare minus tides so low that *Secret*
Beach, where the cave is located, suggested the name, *Secret*
Cave, and so I have referred to it ever since.

What makes the cave so unusual is that once you have walked
into it you find, to your surprise, that the cave has no ceiling and
that you are in an eerily lighted miniature amphitheater. The cave
has a circumference of about 35-40 feet. Since the walls are per-
pendicular, the circumference of the hole at the top is roughly the
same though part of the upper rim has eroded away. The passage, or cave opening through which you pass into the main cave
or amphitheater, is of solid rock.The ceiling of the passage is
about 5 feet so you must lower your head as you pass through
the 20 feet of opening into the amphitheater within. The walls of
the amphitheater, or inner cave, are however, not composed of
rock. Soft eroded soil, fluted in places by rainwater, rises some 80
feet to the opening above. Standing in the amphitheater and
looking up at the sky one feels compelled to look back at the
opening from the sea to check the tide even if the tide was unusually low when one entered but a few minutes earlier. One needs
to be reassured.

From the top of the cave the average hiker feels more comfortable crawling up to, rather than standing at the edge of, the opening and looking straight down to the floor of the cave some 80-90 feet below.

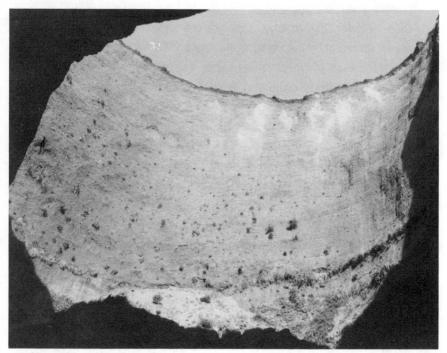

Looking up from within Secret Cave.

Secret Beach[1], the one mile stretch of sand between Sculptured Beach and Point Resistance is itself a place of unusual attraction for those with a sense of adventure.

---

[1] I question the authenticity, or at least the appropriateness, of the name *Secret Beach* for this particular beach at Point Reyes. In fact, I believe that the small beach inside *Point Resistance* was the original *Secret Beach,* a term used to identify this beach by some of the rangers at the original visitor center in the 60's. One of them told me that the beach inside *Point Resistance* was named *Secret Beach* by the rancher who owned the property before the establishment of Point Reyes National Seashore.

There are no access trails leading to Secret Beach from the Coast Trail. The approach to Secret Beach from the south is blocked just north of Kelham Beach by cliffs sheer to the water at lowest of tides. The cliffs rising above Secret Beach are nearly-perpendicular and the few dissecting creeks present no obvious access to the beach below. Thus only from the north, from Sculptured Beach, is there a safe approach though even that one is not obvious.

At the south end of Sculptured Beach there is a prominent off-shore rock, which I call *the Thumb.* Here one comes upon a narrow crack in the headwall dividing Sculptured and Secret beaches.The crack[2], which I call, *the keyhole,* is large enough for a person to pass through. ***However, passage will be blocked or rendered extremely dangerous at high and medium tides. Only at the lowest of tides (check at the Visitor Center for tide information) can one pass through the keyhole safely[3]***.   The passage is but 4 to 5 feet long so that one can easily see through it to the other side. However, the first 20-30 feet of terrain immediately on the Secret Beach side of the keyhole are not seen until one has passed through. These 20-30 feet consist of smooth, deeply embedded rocks which provide excellent, however slippery, *stepping stones* to Secret Beach proper. The mouth of Secret Cave is immediately left towards the land mass as one completes the last rock *stepping stone* from the keyhole. At minus low tides, incidentally, small tide pools form around the rock stepping stones.

---

[2]The crack did not exist until the early 1980's. Erosion opened it. Prior to its appearance a touch and go traverse on steep wet rock was the only way onto Secret Beach.

[3] A low tide of +0.5 or lower makes access from Sculptured Beach to Secret Beach safe unless there are very heavy seas.

Down Secret Beach towards Point Resistance one is aware of nearly sheer and solid rock that is Point Resistance blocking passage a mile ahead. One is also aware of how deserted Secret Beach is.

One of the shower baths along Secret Beach.

In a few places the containing wall of nearly sheer cliffs along Se-cret Beach *are* dissected by small creeks. *I would not recom-*

mend any of these for cross country exit except in emergency. 200 yards or more down Secret Beach from the keyhole there is a waterfall which drops over a smooth, nearly sheer, face rock. The fall, which I call *the first shower bath* is about 10 feet high. Another 100 yards down the beach one comes upon a second waterfall some 12 feet in height. This fall, *the second shower bath* contains more water than the first and tends to shoot out over the cliff and onto the sand below. Both falls are seasonal and begin to lose their gusto or even dry up by July or August. So see them in early spring.

If one continues southeastward down Secret Beach one eventually reaches (1 mile from Secret Cave) the sheer walls of Point Resistance. At this point there is a 35º rock face leading up and out to the Coast Trail by way of a small creek canyon. **The average hiker should not attempt this** – the rock is unstable and the upper portions along the creek have nettle and poison oak. **This is an emergency exit only.**

If one is going to spend an appreciable length of time on Secret Beach one should check the tide tables [4].**The safest exit is back through the keyhole which will close as the tide moves slowly back in. So be alert.**

To reach the keyhole, and thus Secret Beach and Secret Cave, from the Visitor Center at Bear Valley there are three more or less direct routes all leading to Sculptured Beach from which access may be gained, **if the tide is right** , to Secret Beach through the keyhole. From the Visitor Center the approach involving the least

---

4 A tide table booklet is availble at the Visitor Center. **Take one with you.** The booklet lists all the tides for every month of the current year.

amount of climbing is to follow the Bear Valley Trail to where it meets the Coast Trail (4 miles) then turn right –northwestward– to the junction of the Coast Trail and the Sculptured Beach access trail (2.5 miles) then down to Sculptured Beach. A more direct route from the Visitor Center, one involving 1000 feet of ascending and 1200 feet descending, is to follow the Sky Trail (200 yards up the Bear Valley Trail from the Visitor Center). Passing the base of Mt. Wittenberg on the Sky Trail (1.6 miles from the Bear Valley Trailhead) in open country the route turns southwestward to its junction with the Meadow Trail (.4 mile). At this junction the Sky Trail continues straight ahead into the beautiful fir forest of the Inverness Ridge (a branch of the Sky Trail heads hard right towards Sky Camp). Continuing into the forest you'll arrive at the Woodward Valley Trail (.7 mile and erroneously labeled *Woodworth Valley Trail* on the USGS 15' topo map of the National Seashore). Take the Woodward Valley Trail to the Coast Trail (1.8 miles) –perhaps the most beautiful section of trail in the National Seashore– and turn left or southwestward on the Coast Trail to the Sculptured Beach access trail.

From Limantour Beach parking lot one can proceed down the beach to Sculptured Beach (2 miles), **but in a storm or very high tides, the last half mile of that walk can be dangerous.** One can also pick up the Coast Trail some 1000 yards down the beach towards Sculptured Beach and follow along the Coast Trail to Coast Camp. From Coast Camp turn down to the beach and onto Sculptured Beach 800 yards away or continue on the Coast Trail to Sculptured Beach access trail (3/4 mile).

Secret Beach

First keyhole from the south along the Unknown Coast

The Unknown Coast
A Secret Place

"...a stretch of wild, generally inaccessible, coastline with unusual features and discoveries to intrigue the adventurous hiker."

(only for very experienced hikers)

<u>author's note</u>
The information in this chapter has been modified from the information provided in the first edition. *Basic is the recommendation that the Unknown Coast be hiked from* **<u>north to south only</u>** *and not from south to north.*

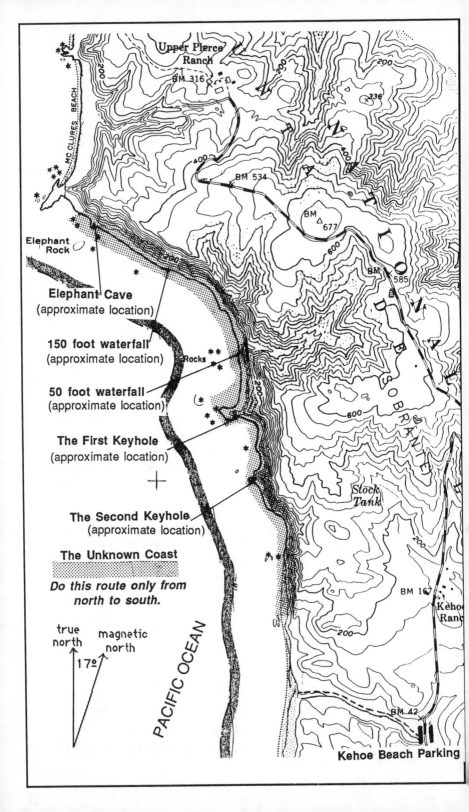

B etween Kehoe Beach and McClures Beach lies a stretch of wild, generally inaccessible, coastline with unusual features and discoveries to intrigue the adventurous hiker. Under rare minus low tide conditions (-0.7 or lower and with calm seas) one can pass through this 2 1/2 miles of varied coastline with its "keyholes", impressive waterfall, empty beaches, magnificent tidepools, brilliant white granite boulders, steep cliffs, and Elephant Cave opposite Elephant Rock.

A look at the tide table for any given year will show why I refer to this stretch of coastline as the Unknown Coast. Since it requires at least a minus 0.2 tide or lower for one to safely travel through this area, since tides this low seldom occur between 8 AM and 5 PM on Saturday, Sunday, or holidays when most hikers prefer to hike, and since the route up or down this coast is characterized by westward extending promontories which are free of the inundation of the returning high tide for a much shorter period than coastline areas farther east, this region is very infrequently traveled. Very few low tides of minus 0.2 or greater fall between 8AM and 5 PM on a Saturday or Sunday when most hikers and explorers are about. Further, many low tides occur in the early hours of the morning or late at night. Of course, if one can plan a trip up the Unknown Coast without regard for the day of the week, then the opportunities are increased. But not much. Considering that most hikers are drawn to the central and southern sections of Point Reyes National Seashore, and that many people, probably most, who come to this section of the Seashore come to enjoy one of the four accessible beaches, Unknown Coast is all the more unknown.

If the low tide is minus 0.7 or lower, plan to be at your starting point—Kehoe Beach or McClures Beach—an hour before the peak of the low tide as indicated in the tide tables. This will enable one to take an unhurried (on account of the eventual turning of the tide) passage along Unknown Coast. The passage around and/or through (keyholes) the four promontories of Unknown Beach, in contrast to the beach areas of the route, is partly underwater (4-18 inches) at low tide.[1] Hence, the promontories will be more quickly and adversely affected by the turning of the tide than the beach areas. *When the tide begins to turn there comes a time when the only way to turn the promontories, which are becoming inundated, is to traverse their steep cliffs 6-15 feet above the water and this is NOT RECOMMENDED.* Whereas on the beaches one has a broad and gentle slope of inland beach to which to retreat. This, of course, is of no great comfort because *when passage around the promontories is closed by the returning high tide one is trapped for at least 5 to 7 hours.* Since the beaches of the Unknown Coast are very narrow there may be little or no room for retreat when the tide approaches or reaches maximum high. *So do not become trappped. Plan to start your trip 30-60 minutes before the time of maximum low tide and you will have sufficient time to make the passage without undue haste.* To make this passage with adequate time to study and enjoy the features described herein, one should do the hike one way only. Thus the return to McClures Beach, the starting point, should be accomplished by use of a pick-up vehicle *(Lock all doors. Roll windows up tight. Lock valuables out of sight, preferably before you arrive at your location. Better yet, leave valuables at home.)* left at the finishing point or by hiking back along the lightly traveled Pierce Point Road. **Do not attempt to return by way of the coast—the three promontories along the route become adversely**

---

[1] Wading through the keyholes of the promontories will be complicated by heavy or even moderately heavy seas which may send occasional waist or chest high waves even at low tide. Once when doing this trek at a minus 0.2 tide during calm seas I was never in deeper than my shins while passing through the keyholes and around the last promontory just below McClures Beach. Whereas in making the passage during a minus 0.6 tide during moderately heavy seas a few waves got me wet to the waist. So study the situation first and proceed cautiously.

affected by the turning of the tide and the inland cliff routes are few and dangerous.

I recommend taking two pairs of "sneakers" (running/tennis type shoes) for the trip - one pair for wading, when it becomes necessary, and the other for the dry sections. Or, divers booties (part of a wet suit) can be taken for the wading, though they don't give protection from submerged rocks as well as "sneakers." Sneakers over divers booties is a fine combination since one has protection from submerged rocks and warmer feet at the same time.[2]

Since the Unknown Coast is narrow and has protruding rock promontories it is especially sensitive to the turning of the tide. It can, thus, be safely hiked only in one direction because the tide will have turned sufficiently as to block a return. The route passes through Elephant Cave at the northern end of the Unknown Coast near McClures Beach. **Under certain conditions the eastern exit to the cave could be blocked with tidal debris, a factor which is best discovered very early in the hike as when coming southward from McClures Beach rather than too late to return safely as when coming northward from Kehoe Beach.** *Therefore, start this hike from McClures Beach.*

On the drive to McClures Beach along Pierce Road drop off your pick-up car(s) at the Kehoe Beach parking area. Then proceed on (about 10 minutes) to McClures Beach parking lot at the end of the road. Hike down roughly 1/2 mile to McClures Beach, then turn southwestward towards the massive rock seen at the far end of the beach some 400 to 500 yards away. As you approach the rock, which jets out into the sea, notice a small notch between it and the rocky headland immediately to the left of the notch. Pass

---

[2] At tides lower than minus 0.08 less wading will be involved.

through the notch onto the small beach beyond - a beach which I'll call the First Beach.

At the southern end of the First Beach is a truncated protrusion of solid rock. Traverse/climb the rock about 2 to 4 feet above the beach and the off-shore low tide water. Descend, then, 2 to 4 feet into the tide pools now visible on the other side of the rocky protrusion just climbed. Wade, cautiously, for 15 to 30 yards (depending on the tide and surf) through tide pools to a boulder field, and, then, onto a small rocky beach beneath sheer cliffs. Some 70 yards beyond the aforementioned tide pools you will be surprised to come upon the mouth of a huge cave - Elephant Cave. The cave is actually a grass covered promontory, with a tunnel reaching deep into the promontory itself towards the headwall of cliffs running along the coastline. At its entrance Elephant Cave is about 30 feet high.It extends some 120-150 feet inward with the ceiling, dripping constantly, gradually lowering. At the eastern end of the cave is an opening some 4 feet high. However, as suggested earlier, it could be closed or blocked with rock, sand and driftwood. Should this condition exist, due to the combination of very high tides and very high seas, turn around and abandon the hike until a later date. There is no safe way around the shoreline from the front of Elephant Cave southward.

Assuming that the eastern end of Elephant Cave is open, as will most likely be the case, proceed through the tunnel to the opening. It consists of a hole at the point where the hollow promontory that is Elephant Cave meets the north-south running cliffs of the Unknown Coast. The descent to a small alcove beach involves a 15-20 foot downward climb over fairly solid rock having an angle of about 55 to 65 degrees. There are plenty of handholds. It will probably be safest to do the descent facing in.

Once on the small alcove beach, head southward along the line of steep cliffs to your left and down a boulder field beach. To your right, standing in the water and facing southwestward, is the Elephant - a perfectly named mass of rock 50 feet above the sea at the shoulders. Proceeding down the boulder field you may see the distinctive black oyster catcher with its black body and red beak. Its screeching may be your first awareness of this seabird. Some 400 to 500 yards from the eastern opening of Elephant Cave you will discover the highest waterfall in Point Reyes National Seashore - an unnamed cascade plunging 125 plus feet over steep rock onto the beach. The fall is seasonal and, thus, is active from roughly December through April or May. In another 50 yards a second waterfall of some 80 to 90 feet plunges onto the beach. This, too, is a seasonal fall of possible shorter duration than the first, inasmuch as it has much less water.

Beyond the waterfalls the route continues on the rocky shoreline and behind a distinctive rock spire 12 to 15 feet in height. Surrounding the spire are numerous tide pools. Deft boulder hopping on generally solid and smooth rock of various sizes and colors brings you upon a field of large granite boulders scattered among darker boulders. The polished granite boulders are beautifully sculptured and, on a sunny day, so brilliantly white that one needs dark glasses to study them.

Beyond the rocky spire with its neighboring tide pools, continue boulder hopping towards a sandy beach, onto which pours another spectacular seasonal waterfall roughly 50 to 60 feet in height. I have named this sandy beach "Second Beach" and the falls "Ribbon Falls", for reasons which will be obvious to the viewer. On a windy afternoon in winter and spring a fine spray will swirl around the base of the cliffs. By summer the fall will have dwindled down to a trickle. Second Beach is entirely wild and empty. Seldom does one see another person on this wildest coast of the Seashore.

Moving on, and looking ahead from Ribbon Falls, you will observe a rocky promontory jetting into the sea with no discernible route around or through it. Nonetheless, continue hiking along until the rocky headwall of the promontory is encountered at its junction with the north-south line of cliffs. It is here, on the rocky cliffs above, that I first saw red-faced cormorants with their blackish-green feathers around the neck and white spots towards the rear of the body at Point Reyes.

Wade cautiously through shallow tide pools cautiously until an obvious "keyhole" opening is encountered some 40 yards from the point where one leaves the beach to begin wading. This, "First Keyhole", is a short tunnel leading to tide pools at the base of the west facing cliffs on the other side of the promontory through which one has just passed via the First Keyhole. Wade, now, in 12 inch to 24 inch tide pools, *exercising caution and keeping an eye on the sea.* Within 30 to 40 yards the west facing headwall turns eastward, and you will observe a beach just beyond the final 40 to 50 feet of tide pools. This, the "Third Beach", is, like the Second Beach, generally deserted. And, as with the First and Second Beaches , overland exit would be very dangerous, if not impossible, because of the steep and unstable cliffs.

Some 600 straightline yards from the point where you step out of the tide pools onto the sands of the Third Beach, you can see a truncated rock promontory jetting only slightly into the sea. As you approach this next, and last, obstacle you will notice a small hole in the north wall of the stubby promontory in question. When you see the hole, head down the hard packed sands of the Third Beach to the rocky north facing headwall as it leads you westward through the tide pools some 30 yards. Note the mussel covered solid rock cliffs to your left. Climb up for about 10 to 12 feet, on solid ledges for foot and handholds, to a mussel covered platform. Observe the "Second Keyhole" some 75 feet away and to your left. Descend, preferably by facing in, on mussel covered ledges some 10 feet to a level field of boulders and tide pools. The Second Keyhole, which is just wide enough to get through, is now 35 feet away. All that remains is to boulder hop slightly upward to the keyhole and then squeeze through.

Once through the Second Keyhole you immediately encounter a boulder field some 200 yards or more in length. A few of the boulders may have moss and/or kelp material on them and will, as a result, be slippery. It is important to exercise caution and move slowly. The occasional tide pools will provide relief from boulder hopping, but be cautious about wading if you cannot see the bottoms of the pools. They usually won't be very deep, but some could be above the knees.

Once past the boulder field you touch down on the sands of Kehoe Beach for an easy saunter along wet and hard packed sand. Follow down the beach past three huge semi-cliffs, which are about 20 to 25 feet above their bases on the beach, past embedded rock outcrops jetting well out towards the edge of the low tide surf, and on to the Kehoe Beach access trail. The trail itself is not seen from the beach, but 100 or so yards from reaching a prominent (in winter and spring) stream which emerges onto the sands of Kehoe Beach, notice a white dune which is usually packed with footprints. Head inland for about 150 to 175 yards, climb the gentle slopes of the dune for 40 yards, and discover the trail which, in .6 mile, will lead you to the Kehoe Beach parking area and your pick up vehicle(s).

The Unknown Coast provides a short adventure filled with the excitement of discovery and the experience of wild beauty in a place few people ever see. It is an adventure in any season of the year though the two waterfalls will be active in the spring.

Dogwood in full bloom – mid April

Dogwood & Dawn Redwood
A Secret Place

"The white dogwood flower is resplendent in sunlight or moonlight, and in spring there is no flowering bush or tree to match it for dazzling beauty at Point Reyes National Seashore."

"The Dawn Redwood at Point Reyes stands barely 700 yards from the Bear Valley Trailhead – its existence something of a secret, known only to a few people."

Dawn Redwood

L ess than a half mile from the Bear Valley Trailhead - from the gate dividing the parking area from the Bear Valley Trail - is a 40 to 45 foot dogwood tree. It stands on a small meadow across the creek running from Divide Meadow through the eastern portion of Bear Valley to Tomales Bay. 100 feet away, and closer to the Bear Valley Trail (60 feet), is a tree whose ancestors florished 30 million years ago in North America - a Dawn Redwood.

The dogwood should hardly be a secret, but over the 27 years I've known Bear Valley I've seldom seen anyone stopped along the trail to observe the tree 150 feet away. The reason, perhaps, that the dogwood tree usually goes unnoticed is because it is in bloom for only about two months - from early March to late April or early May. The small meadow on which the tree stands was once a site containing two or three small buildings. The dogwood stands at the west end of the meadow. When in bloom there is no mistaking it, for it has the appearance of being covered with a fresh and heavy snowfall! The white dogwood flower (six white petals, 2 to 4 inches long) is resplendent in sunlight or moonlight, and in spring there is no flowering bush or tree to match it for dazzling beauty at Point Reyes National Seashore.

Look for the dogwood 650 to 700 yards from the unpaved parking lot from the Bear Valley Trail. Some 680 yards from the gate one encounters a small tributary coming from the right (a brown metal stake marks the the tributary) and passing under a culvert. Just before and just past this tributary one can view the dogwood. Crossing the creek to examine the tree is no problem except during a heavy rainy season when one might have to wade.

A Dawn Redwood (Metasequoia), planted around 1949, may be

observed 60 feet from the Bear Valley Trail as one looks across the creek from a point 40 yards past the aforementioned tributary. The tree is about 55 feet tall. Its reddish bark is thin and slightly fissured, thus it does not, in its bark resemble the Coast Redwood or Sempervirens. Unlike other redwoods, the Dawn Redwood is deciduous, shedding its needles in the fall and budding out anew in the spring. Characteristically, the branches are slightly ascending, as opposed to the horizontal branches of the Coast Redwood (Sequoia Sempervirens). Upon examination however, I did notice that this Dawn Redwood had,in its lower section, branches that were horizontal. Only higher up did the branches ascend.

The genus Metasequoia is a conifer which was widely distributed over the northern hemisphere in past ages. It was considered to have become extinct some 20,000,000 years ago. In 1944 the exciting discovery of a living Metasequoia by T. Wang, a forester employed by the Ministry of Agriculture of the then Chinese Nationalist Government, was reported. He had come upon the large tree near the village of Mo-tao-chi, in the province of Szechuan in Central China. Consultation with Dr. H. H. Hu, director of Fan Memorial Institute of Peking, resulted in the discovery that the cones and foliage were identical to fossil specimens of the Metasequoia. Until this, the only evidence of Dawn Redwoods were fossilized remains of the trees from the Eocene era, 60 million years ago, in Siberia, Alaska, Spitzbergen, Greenland and the arctic islands of Canada. Somewhat more recently (30 million years ago) fossilized Metasequoia of the Neocene age had been discovered in Oregon, California, Germany, Switzerland, Manchuria and Japan. It was considered that the last trees died out as the earth's climate changed 20 million years ago.

Excited by the reports of the discovery of living metasequoia, Dr. Ralph W. Chaney of the University of California at Berkeley Department of Paleontology, the leading expert on living fossils and redwoods, traveled to China to study the trees and establish the accuracy of the discovery.

In 1948 small trees raised from seeds brought from China were planted in the Pacific Northwest. Since then thousands of Metasequoia have been distributed in the United States, Europe and Asia.

The Dawn Redwood at Point Reyes stands barely 700 yards from the Bear Valley Trailhead - its existence something of a secret, known only to a few people.

For additional information on the Metasequoia write:
Save the Redwoods League
114 Sansome Street
San Francisco, CA 94104

Wildcat Beach and Double Point from Wildcat Beach Overlook

Wildcat Beach Overlook
A Secret Place & A Magic Moment

"...at sunset, on a clear starry night, or beneath the full moon the scene is nothing less than mystical."

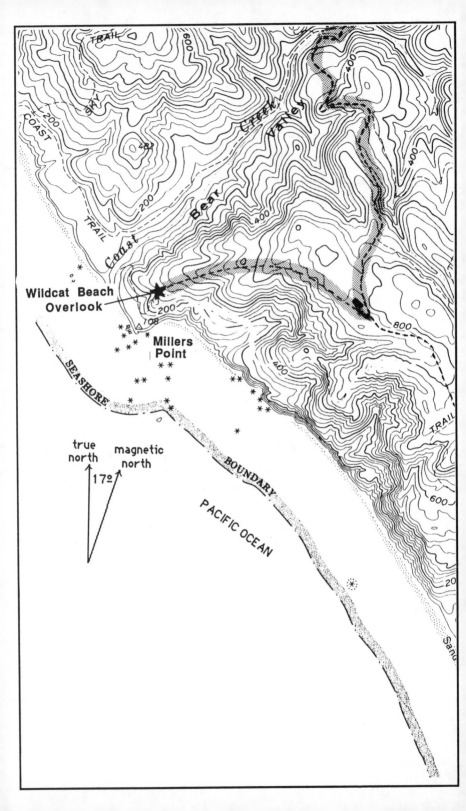

There is a little known panorama at Point Reyes National Seashore which is inspiring on the most ordinary of days. However, at sunset, on a clear starry night, or beneath the full moon the scene is nothing less than mystical. Here all sorrows are erased, all tragedies redeemed. In 27 years of exploring Point Reyes National Seashore over and over again one of the two most aesthetically sublime moments I have experienced in this benign region was here beneath a full moon in May. Since that initial experience I have returned to the spot – *the Wildcat Beach Overlook* (my name) – many times to experience again, and somehow anew, that indescribable beauty of land and sea by moonlight.

To reach *Wildcat Beach Overlook* most directly take the Bear Valley Trail from the Visitor Center to its junction with the Coast Trail 4 miles from the Visitor Center. Turn left, or southward on the Coast Trail. At this junction the Coast Trail becomes a bona fide trail as distinct from the old ranch road that is the Bear Valley Trail and the Coast Trail itself if one was to turn right onto the northern portion of the trail. The Coast Trail's southern turn is marked, at this writing, by a small post with the symbol of a hiker and a directional arrow. Within 75 yards of the post the Coast Trail crosses Coast Creek on a foot bridge and then turns towards Miller Point and the sea 200-250 yards away. 200 yards of generally level hiking brings one onto a broad and grassy shelf with a view of the sea and the Arch Rock Overlook less than 100 yards away. Coast Trail now turns gradually southward and parallel to the Coastline, then switches back to begin a 200-250 yard 15º climb to a rocky flat where the trail levels off briefly before switching back to begin climbing again. Standing on the rocky flat, from where there is a magnificent northward view towards Limantour Beach, Drakes Beach, and Point Reyes itself, turn so that you are facing the Coast Trail as it switches back and resumes its upward path in open country. Then look further to the right by about 75º from the line of the Coast Trail to a small knoll or hill 130 yards or more away and at about the same elevation as the rocky flat on which you are standing. Head, cross country, through the grass to the top of the hill. Once on the top of the hill continue, in the same direction, over it and down, in 10-15 yards, to a flat area that suggests an old wagon road except that it is only about 50 yards long. This is Wildcat Beach Overlook. Before and below you is a sweeping view of the entire Wildcat Beach, Alamere Falls, and the northern point of Double Point. Westward, 30 miles out to the sea, the Farallon Islands can be seen on a clear day when the sea sparkles to all horizons. All of the southern half of Drakes Bay lies before you. Far to the south the Coastal areas of San Mateo County are discernible.

At sunset, beneath a full or near full moon, or at moonset this location affords a heightened aesthetic experience, a truly magic moment.

Wildcat Beach at low tide. Southward view toward Double Point.

Alamere Falls

Alamere Falls
A Secret Place

"One can sit next to the falls with feet dangling over the edge of the cliff and watch ocean breakers and whitecaps, seagulls and sandpipers, hikers and picnickers while marveling at the power and beauty of Alamere Falls."

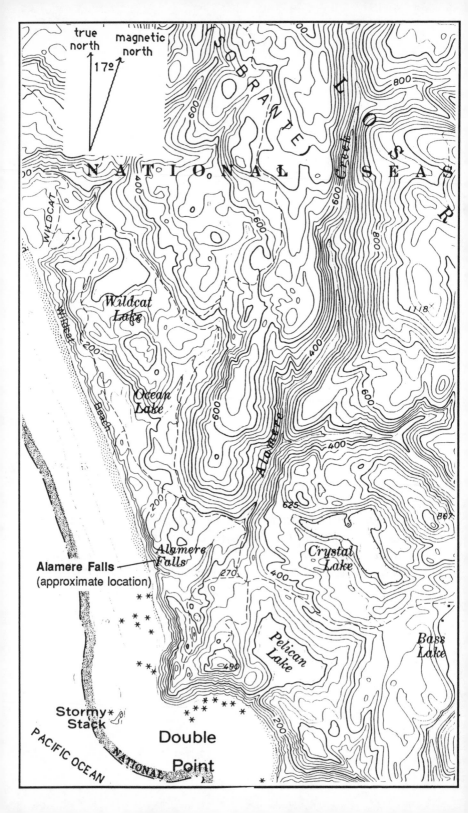

Alamere Falls
(approximate location)

A *lamere Falls,* 1 mile south of Wildcat Beach from Wildcat Camp, is well known. On a given weekend day hikers up from Palomarin Trailhead (5.6 miles distant) out of Bolinas, or out of Fire Brooks Trailhead (7 miles distant), or coming down from Bear Valley Trailhead (7 miles) converge on *Alamere Falls.* Overnight campers at Wildcat Camp usually walk down to the falls after setting up camp on the afternoon of their arrival.

The falls drop 40 feet straight over a low cliff onto the beach below. At the cliff edge the falls are 15-25 feet wide depending on the season of the year and the season's rainfall. Fed by Alamere Creek, which rises nearly 1000 feet above and 2.25 miles beyond the sea, the waterfall is active all year 'round. It has the greatest volume of water of all the 10 or more Waterfalls (most of them seasonal) at Point Reyes. Alamere Falls can be seen, most readily on a clear afternoon, from the west facing hills above Coast Camp as a stubby white ribbon seemingly attached to the distant earth colored cliffs running northward from Double Point.

Alamere Falls are most impressive immediately after, or even during, heavy rains which occur in winter and spring. The sound of the water smashing onto embedded rocks at the base of the falls becomes, in these conditions, very impressive. From the base of the falls Alamere Creek cuts a trough 12-15 inches deep and 10-18 inches wide as it makes a final surge to the sea.

A fine picture of the waterfalls can be obtained, with wide angle lens from the shoreline or, in a calm sea, 6 to 8 feet out in the water. In March or April squalls sometimes occur amid the broken clouds of a spring rain. In such conditions, and in mid to late afternoon with the sun facing the waterfall and the Olema Ridge to the east, the conditions are right for rainbows. Patience and luck will play a big factor in one's being at Alamere Falls at the right time for a rainbow but, even without a rainbow, the falls are particularly photogenic on a day with broken clouds at late afternoon. By moonlight, especially after a big rain, the falls are magical.

One can gain access to the top of the falls to witness the after rain surge. Facing the falls dead center look 30-40 yards to the left and notice a strong suggestion of a path 30 feet up through fine scree. The first 15 feet do not involve any real exposure to anything more than getting skinned up at the very worst. The last 4

Alamere Falls & Alamere Creek

feet involve a slightly more exposed drop. However the hand and footholds are generally good and once past this last 4 feet off the route follow either of the two clearly marked footpaths to the top of the falls 50 feet away. A safer, but more circuitous route, is to break off the Coast Trail on a discernible footpath within 100 yards of Alamere Creek on the south side. The footpath moves west towards the sea in open country. The place of the footpath's departure from the Coast Trail is at a point where the Coast Trail makes a semi hairpin west to east turn. The footpath becomes crude and becomes a kind of staircase[1] down a 50º cliff for 12-15 feet to the stream bed of Alamere Creek as it makes a final cascade 60 feet from the edge of the cliff. Cross the stream, with a step or jump depending on the volume of water, and you'll be standing on a natural platform of relatively flat rock across which Alamere Creek makes its last run to the edge of the cliff before falling free to the beach below.

One can sit next to the falls with feet dangling over the edge of the cliff and watch ocean breakers and whitecaps, seagulls and sandpipers, hikers and picnickers while marveling at the power and beauty of Alamere Falls.

---

[1] Steps have been cut in the cliff. Face in or out while descending – whichever is more comfortable.

Female Tule elk

Tomales Point
A Secret Place & A Magic Moment

*"...a little known place from where one can watch
two magnificent bays meet with each other and
the Pacific Ocean in a carnival of surging and
churning water."*

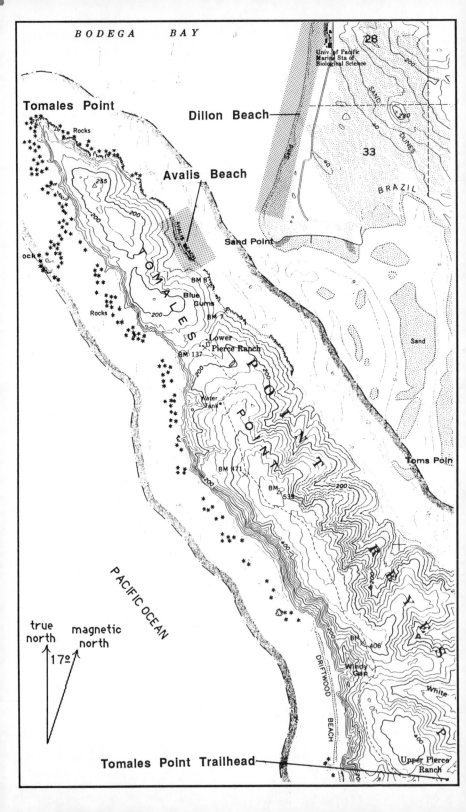

The northern tip of the Point Reyes peninsula, which is accessible from the Tomales Point Trailhead at the site of Pierce Ranch, is known for the Tule Elk which were returned to the Point Reyes region in the 1970's after more than a half century's absence.[1] And 200 yards west of Tomales Point Trailhead is McClures Beach Trailhead from where over one hundred picnickers and sunbathers head .6 mile to the beach on any decent Saturday or Sunday from April to late October. However, what most people, including seasoned hikers, don't known is that 5 miles northward there is a little known place from where one can watch two magnificent bays meet with each other and the Pacific Ocean in a carnival of surging and churning water. And what even fewer people know is that there is a 30 day period in spring when this region provides a dazzling display of yellow wild flowers of all varieties, a display unequaled anywhere in Point Reyes National Seashore!

To Reach Tomales Point Trailhead drive on Sir Frances Drake Boulevard. off Highway 101 starting at the San Anselmo turn-off as one heads north on 101. Continue on Sir Francis Drake to Olema in West Marin County. At Olema Sir Francis Drake Boulevard. coincides, briefly, with state Highway 1. Turn right, on both roads, travel through Inverness, and proceed to a point some 2 miles beyond Inverness where Francis Drake Blvd. meets the Pierce Ranch Road. Take Pierce Ranch road by keeping right (Sir Francis Drake Boulevard. veers left towards Drakes Beach and the lighthouse at Point Reyes itself). In about 9 miles from this junction the Pierce Ranch Road, running through pastoral countryside, comes to an end at Tomales Point Trailhead. A small

---

1 I have heard two accounts as to the departure of the Tule Elk from Point Reyes National Seashore shortly after 1900: 1) The original herd left in a drought and headed north by swimming the mouth of Tomales Bay! 2) The herd, reduced in number by hunters, departed overland starting somewhere off the south end of Tomales Bay

parking area, beneath sprawling cypress trees and adjacent to the old Pierce Ranch, is found here. Allow 2 1/4- 2 1/2 hours driving from San Francisco or Berkeley.

The Tomales Point Trail winds up and down on the broad crest of a narrowing peninsula which is gradually pinched off by Tomales Bay and the Pacific Ocean where they merge with Bodega Bay and cut off the peninsula. The country is open and covered mostly with coyote brush and bush lupine. Follow the trail, watching for Tule Elk which may sometimes be seen almost immediately – 200 yards from the parking area. Continue for about 3 miles from the parking area to a point where it reaches a depressed area marked by a small clump of cypress trees. This is the site of Lower Pierce Ranch where nothing remains of the buildings once situated here and where the trail changes from old ranch road to a bona fide trail or footpath. The trail begins to fade away as one follows northward through increasingly sandy soil and up a gentle but extended slope, covered with bush lupine and coyote brush. A semblance of trail may yet be found, even a hint of an old ranch road, but eventually you're pretty much on your own through the maze of 3-4 feet coyote brush and bush lupine. However, passage is not difficult since there are usually plenty of gaps between the bushes. One is aware of barren Bird Rock to the west and, not infrequently, startled rabbit underfoot. At the crest of the gentle and extended rise from the site of Lower Pierce Ranch one begins a very gradual descent through the low bushes towards yet unseen Tomales Point and the waters of Bodega Bay which are, by now, partly visible. To the right, or northeast, Dillons Beach is now visible on the east shore of Tomales Bay (those colorful objects you might see in the sand dunes at Dillons Beach are hang gliders). Finally, the peninsula narrows, the bushes begin giving way to grassy slopes, and you are there at land's end. Possibly, if there are swells of any size you'll hear buoy bells ringing at the mouth of Tomales Bay. Fishing boats will most likely be seen bobbing up and down in the swells, or, on a foggy day, seeming to float in an ethereal mist. Pelicans may buzz your grassy knoll as they shortcut from Tomales Bay to the Pacific Ocean or in the opposite direction. Beyond the watery crossroads of Tomales Bay, Bodega Bay, and the Pacific Ocean you can make out Bodega and Bodega Head (where once PG&E planned a nuclear reactor!). In April – all this and flowers too!

From about mid April (it will vary a little every year depending on the amount of rainfall) to mid May is the peak time for spring flowers – golden flowers – at the northern tip of the 5 mile peninsula between Tomales Point Trailhead and Tomales Point. One April my party of hikers counted over 21 different kinds of yellow/golden wild flowers.[2] The flowers were so thick, especially the goldfields, in that final cross country mile to Tomales Point we had to pick our steps to avoid stepping on them. The dominant flower was the yellow bush lupine. Together with the coyote brush the bush lupine stood 2 1/2 to 4 1/2 feet high thus affording bouquets which were almost at eye level. Necessarily our hiking pace was reduced to less than 1 mile per hour as we sauntered through the garden of yellow flowers sniffing, studying, taking pictures, and just glorying in the incredible display of delicate beauty. And the aroma permeated the warm spring air nearly to the point of being overpowering.

Yet another little known spot here at the very tip of the Point Reyes peninsula, a spot barely one mile from Tomales Point, is

---

2 Predominant were yellow lupine, goldfield, poppies, fiddleneck buttercups, and cream cups.

Avalis Beach. Located on the west shore of Tomales Bay this beach is the best beach on the west shore of Tomales Bay from Tomales Point to White Gulch. Because it is located away from the Pacific Ocean on sheltered Tomales Bay, Avalis Beach receives less wind. And the surf is much more gentle than the Pacific Ocean surf. One can reach Avalis Beach from Tomales Point by retracing the route about halfway back to Lower Pierce Ranch then turning westward to find a shallow creek bed emptying towards Tomales Bay. Stay out of the overgrown creek bed keeping along the sandy slopes north of it. The only difficulty will be a short, less than sheer, bank of 4-6 feet which must be descended to the beach. Caution and cooperation within the group will suffice, and you will have your beach entirely to yourselves in all probability.

There is yet another unique aesthetic experience to be enjoyed along the Tomales Point Trail – or just off it. On many a typical spring afternoon the westerlies come racing in from the open sea and set the tall grasses along the trail to wildly dancing. Moving northward on the trail continue up past Windy Gap, which is slightly more than a mile from the parking lot, to any point along the trail once it has leveled off. Leave the trail to your left (westward) through the blowing grasses and continue for some 150-300 yards to a point where you have a commanding view southward. McClure Beach, Elephant Rock, Kehoe Beach, the Great Beach, and Point Reyes itself should all be visible. Find a comfortable spot to sit and watch both the swaying grasses near at hand and the patchwork of choppy waves far below on the Pacific Ocean. Watch the waves crest, break, and crest again in rapid succession. Or lie back and listen to the sound of the gusty blasts as they seem to shake even the earth beneath you. Naturally this experience is the more enjoyable if you are warmly dressed –polypropylene underwear beneath down jacket, wind pants, along with wool socks and cap.

Finally, try a hike – or short walk – at Tomales Point under a waning moon. Start when the moon rises at 3 am, somewhere in its last quarter. Pick a day when the weather promises to be favorable and begin the hike or walk at about 3:30 am or 4:00 am after the moon has had time to move above the eastern horizon. Consider taking breakfast so that you can have one of the most unusual morning meals you've ever had.

In the meanwhile the faint light of the moon will be gradually replaced by twilight. Gradually the vague forms on either side of the trail will now become distinct as bushes, rock outcrops, and even Tule Elk! The stars will begin to dash away in rapid succession as a glowing light silhouettes the hill far to the east. And you find yourself in twilight here on a grassy hilltop between the open sea and Tomales Bay which are now beginning to take form. The still air is fragrant with the sweet aroma of dew moistened grass. In the silence, which is so utter that you can hear it, you will know why you came. And why you will come again.

Once, when roaming these gentle hills along the Tomales Point Trail in the twilight of summer I stopped to become absorbed in the beauty spread about at my feet in all directions. As I did so I was startled to hear the faint sound of a flute! I recognized the tune immediately but couldn't think of the name. Then the words came up to me as the distant flutist repeated and I hummed along softly – "though the heart be weary, sad the day and long, still to us at twilight comes love's old song, comes love's old sweet song."

Elephant Rock

Drama at Elephant Rock
A Secret Place & A Magic Moment

*"On a clear windy day or in the midst of a full
scale Pacific storm huge ocean swells blast
against the rock sending scores of white spears of
seawater skyrocketing into the air."*

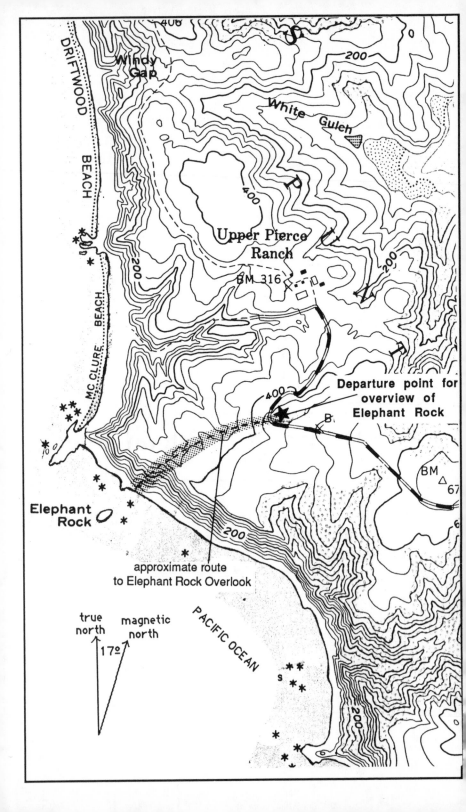

E *lephant Rock,* immediately south of Mc Clure Beach, is best seen as an "elephant" on the hills overlooking the sea. When Elephant Rock and the sea join battle they can put on one of the most dramatic displays mother nature can provide at Point Reyes National Seashore. On a clear windy day or in the midst of a full scale Pacific storm huge ocean swells blast against the rock sending scores of white spears of seawater skyrocketing into the air. Gradually the white spears lose momentum and slowly loop over in a lazy crescent to plunge softly into the sea in a fine spray. Some swells are larger than others, of course, and one has the joy of anticipation, while waiting to see if the next blast of sea water will shoot even higher into the air. All the while the viewer is safely perched some 200 feet above the sea and, direct line, 1000 feet distance from the spectacle.

The vantage point above Elephant Rock is reached by traveling cross country over the open hills immediately southwest of the point where Pierce Road takes a sharp descending near hairpin turn one half mile from Tomales Point Trailhead. You will find, in places, enough space along the south shoulder of the road to park off the road. The USGS Tomales quadrangle map shows a bench mark (BM534) a few hundred yards from the aforementioned bend in the road. Just east of the sharp bend in the road a half mile's walk due west over grass covered hills will take you to a viewpoint with a commanding panorama of the Pacific Ocean and Elephant Rock[1]. An approximately 325 foot descent is involved over that half mile walk to the edge of the cliff. *Do not attempt to climb down any cliff because they are*

---

[1] Elephant Rock will be easily dsitinquished from other large rocks nearby. It looks very much like an Elephant facing out to sea.

not only steep but composed of very unstable rock. The only reasonably safe route to the beach is described in the chapter on Elephant Cave.

If it is a clear and windy day for your adventure wear warm clothing including wool and/or thick down. Don't judge the temperature by how you feel 30 seconds after stepping out of your car. You must be prepared to sit in a strong cold wind for 30 to 60 minutes to fully experience the ocean spectacle at Elephant Rock. Wearing polypropylene underwear, or its equivalent, wool pants, wool sweater, down jacket, wool cap, and wool mittens or gloves, you will be protected from the cold. *If it is a Pacific storm you seek for your adventure at Elephant Rock wear rain gear.* Include waterproof cover for head, hands and feet (rain hat or, better, a hood *must* be securely attached). Winds may be fierce (50mph+) and, while they will not blow you over, they will make walking sometimes awkward and, most serious, they will chill you should you become wet due to inadequate rain gear. If any member of your party becomes wet and/or cold the automobile will be only a half mile away so problems with exposure can be quickly dealt with. However, don't let the close proximity of your auto be cause for complacency and thus cause you delay in returning to the auto in the event someone in the party is getting wet and/or uncomfortably cold.

All these words of caution are not designed to frighten, but to clearly advise you as to how to enjoy one of nature's great dramas in comfort and safety. Properly clothed, you will be dry, warm, and ready for a supremely unique experience.

Elephant Rock from the rocky beach near Elephant Cave.

Wildcat Beach

Alone in the Wilderness
A Magic Moment

"Alone in the wilderness I feel how so much of what we experience in the urban world is superficial and pedantic, while what we experience in the wilderness is essential and profound."

Looking westward to the Olema Ridge

I have hiked in Point Reyes National Seashore on the average of 20 times a year since a time before the National Seashore was created in the early 1960's I've hiked in groups, with friends, with the women in my life, and alone. These situations are all quite different even though they all have a common setting. Each situation has its own special quality, its own uniqueness. Of the four situations, walking alone at Point Reyes, or in any natural environment, provides by far the best opportunity to fully experience the beauty and wonder of wilderness. Hence this chapter on walking alone.

In any group outing to a natural region, small group or large group, the inevitable social interactions tend to distract the attention of the individual. Therefore, one is less aware of his or her surroundings while in conversation with others. Exceptions to this situation exist, or course, when the group is concentrating its attention on a particular item of biologic or aesthetic interest. However, it has been my experience that, unless a group is part of a class studying some aspect of natural history, the predominant conversations have to do with matters unrelated to the surroundings. This inevitable tendency may be good and necessary in itself but, unfortunately, it distracts people from the experience they presumably sought when they decided to take an excursion to the wilderness[1].

Long ago I discovered that when walking alone in the wilderness I am infinitely more aware of my surroundings. And I always

---

[1] I consider Point Reyes National Seashore as much *wilderness* as Kings Canyon National Park, for example. It's proximity to urban areas does not significantly change the natural environment itself in Point Reyes National Seashore.

discover that in my solo experiences I go beyond mere *awareness* to something deeper at one particular moment on an excursion.

On repeated trips to Point Reyes, and other wilderness regions where I have been many times, I experience anew this deeper sensitivity. It renews me. It leaves me feeling joyful, even inspired. I have a sense of kinship with the natural environment around me. It is as if I know each tree, meadow, flower, animal. And they know me. I sometimes give a salutation to any particular natural object or to the entire area that I am experiencing be it Point Reyes, Gates of the Arctic, the High Sierra, the Southern Alps of New Zealand, or "anywhere that's wild". I sense that Plato was right when he said that Beauty was not a subjective experience in the eye of the beholder but, instead, an absolute force or cosmic entity which manifests itself through many media including nature. Alone in the wilderness I sometimes experience a sense of infinity – a feeling which I cannot put in words. I also have, at particular and heightened moments, a sense of a vague all pervading benign force which is somehow conscious and reaches out to include me. Passing particular waterfalls, meadows, or beaches, which I have experienced many times before, I have a sense of newness. It is as if I am experiencing these scenes for the first time even though I know them well. I have learned, intellectually, that I have a kinship with nature but sitting alone before a Point Reyes sunset I *feel* the kinship. Alone in the wilderness I feel how so much of what we experience in the urban world is superficial and pedantic while what we can experience in the wilderness is essential and profound. From my limited experience all things seem to begin and then, to end; but on a flower scented hill at any time of day I can gain a sense, a feel, of something eternal. I come away with a feeling that all sorrows will be erased, all tragedies redeemed. Life seems infinitely worth living.I can often bring on these experiences at will by simply stopping to watch and listen for a period of time. More often, however, a particular scene is so exquisitely beautiful, as I move along the trail, that I am compelled to stop and become absorbed. All that is required for the magnificent interaction between one's self and the natural environment is for one to be open, receptive. And when alone one is much more receptive.

I do not wish to imply that alone in the wilderness one will inevitably be in a heightened state of awareness the whole day. Since it is partly a matter of will, of deciding to be receptive, one has some control. I find that I go in and out of this deeper state throughout the day. Sometimes I am a geologist examining rock formations. Sometimes I am a biologist, a photographer, or in a brief conversation with someone else hiking along the trail. I have no idea what percentage of the day is spent in or or of this state of communion with my surroundings. I never concern myself with this except, sometimes, in the first half hour or so of a solo hike when my mind seems to be stuck on all the doings of my urban world. In this situation I make repeated efforts to shut out these concerns for agendas, meetings, appointments, and projects so I can be with the natural environment. As soon as I successfully cast off the urban baggage I just *go with the flow* of my experiences of my surroundings.

The implication of all this is not that one has to be a confirmed mystic to have deep, even profound, experiences in the wilderness. The recreating, self and life confirming, experiences of the wilderness are known to a variety of people with a variety of background. As a wilderness guide for 32 years I have had the pleasure of introducing hundreds of people to the wilderness –

students, housewives, psychiatrists, executives, entertainers, senior citizens, on and on. I have witnessed their reactions and heard their testimonies. Sometimes the process is slow and painful depending on the particular wilderness region experienced, the length of visitation, and the individual. But sooner or later (sooner at Point Reyes)[2], the individual is touched, deeply. On an evaluation form an anonymous student wrote, after a first wilderness experience, one which involved a good deal of structured solo time, "the security of eternity is overwhelming."

The solo experience, for those who are a little hesitant, can be initiated by breaking off from the other members of a group excursion and continuing 50-100 yards in front or behind. Or by sitting alone at lunch or during any prolonged rest. Some leaders of groups, myself included, structure an opportunity for individuals of a group to walk alone for 30-60 minutes. Individuals can walk a certain section of well defined trail 1, 2, 3, or more minutes apart after instructions are given. Then the leader or assistant goes ahead to rendezvous point while the assistant leader acts as a sweep. I find that the solo walk period is consistently the most impactful part of any group trip which I lead.

For those – men as well as women – who are reluctant to hike alone, solo hiking on clearly marked trails while participating on a group excursion should not be intimidating. In this situation someone is 1,2, or 3 minutes ahead and another person 1 to 3 minutes behind. Sitting a hundred feet or more away from the

---

[2] I have experienced in myself and observed in others that rugged and/or very remote wilderness region can be somewhat intimidating in the initial period of a wilderness trip for the uninitiated. Point Reyes is pastoral, gentle, and anything but remote.

group during lunch or during a break should also be comfortable enough. In time those who break themselves in by this manner may become willing to start out with short solo walks leading to yet longer ones on their own.

As already indicated one does not have to go alone into Point Reyes National Seashore or into any wilderness region to experience the natural world on a deeper level. However, the interaction between the individual and wilderness is one to one, a private experience which happens, I believe, mostly in spite of the group rather than because of it. Even when no solo time is deliberately taken there will be at least a few private moments, such as when a person awakens in the night under a canopy of stars, shared between an individual and the natural environment. The intensive experience of the wilderness is, then essentially a solo experience.

John Muir wrote, "Every day was a holiday and all the world lay before me". The effervescent joy that inspired that sentence came from the experience wilderness, a private interaction between one man and the compelling beauty around him.

Woodward Valley Trail as seen from the junction of the Sky Trail

Panoramic Hill
A Magic Moment

"By moonlight the scene is enchanting, as a million moonspangles dance into the night while the occasional lights of distant ships wink on and off and the faint sound of breakers provide nocturnal music in the otherwise absolute silence of the night."

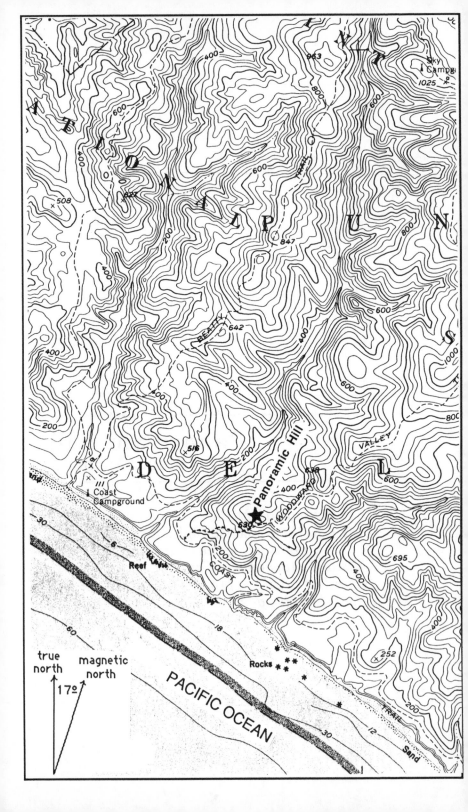

The best view of Drakes Bay anywhere in Point Reyes National Seashore is not from the highest hills, Mount Vision, Point Reyes Hill, or Mount Wittenberg. Nor is it from the eastern tip of Point Reyes itself. The best panorama is found, instead, on an unnamed hill 530 feet above the sea, one-half mile from the sands of Sculptured Beach, and opposite a point nearly dead center in Drakes Bay. *Panoramic Hill* (my name) is 5 1/2 miles straight line from the southern tip of Drakes Bay at Double Point and 6 7/8 miles straight line from the containing arm of Point Reyes itself. Standing on the summit of the hill one looks straight up Limantour Beach, across the opening of Drakes Estero, along the sweeping arc of Drakes Beach to land's end opposite Chimney Rock at Point Reyes itself. Then, turning the opposite direction, one views the shore of Secret Beach as it runs smack into the unyielding Point Resistance, then Kelham Beach, Arch Rock Overlook at Miller Point, Wildcat Beach, even Alamere Falls, and, finally the northern tip of Double Point 5 1/2 miles distance. The two panoramas present 17 miles of cliffs, beaches, and waterfalls. Behind the beach line most of Limantour Estero, part of Drakes Estero, the high cliffs which characterize Drakes Bay, and the low lying land mass connecting Point Reyes beach with Point Reyes itself are clearly visible on a good day.

The scenery from Panoramic Hill is sometimes dramatic as on a day of broken clouds or on a day when a low lying coastal fog, having hidden the beach and areas immediately inland, begins slowly to evaporate. By moonlight the scene is enchanting, as a million moonspangles dance into the night while the occasional lights of distant ships wink on and off and the faint sound of breakers provide nocturnal music in the otherwise absolute silence of the night.

The eastward view from the hill top is one of wooded ridges and occasional patches of brush covered hills, radiant in the midday sun of spring or summer or somber and melancholy under a heavy overcast.

Panoramic Hill is just off the Woodward Valley Trail. On the USGS 7 1/2 minute topographical Inverness quadrangle map the hill is indicated as located immediately (100 yards) northwest of a point where the trail, having suddenly brought you to a full view of Drakes Bay, turns sharply northwest towards a hill some 50-60 vertical feet above you as you come upon the expansive view. The hill's elevation, 530 feet, is printed on the 7 1/2 minute USGS Inverness topographical map and on the 19x15 minute USGS Point Reyes topographical map.

To reach Panoramic Hill from Bear Valley Trailhead pick up the Sky Trail 300 yards from the Bear Valley Trailhead parking lot. Follow the Sky Trail to the Woodward Valley Trail and travel on for 1.3 miles on the Woodward Valley Trail to Panoramic Hill.

From the Limantour Beach parking lot take the Coast Trail, or hike along the beach, first to Coast Camp then to the junction of Coast Trail and Woodward Valley Trail. Proceed up the open switchbacks of the Woodward Valley Trail for about 1/2 mile to Panoramic Hill.

The short route off the Woodward Valley Trail to the hilltop is most obvious when coming west down the trail from the Sky Trail junction. As soon as the hill is clearly in view, just as one comes upon the expansive view of Drakes Bay, continue for about 100 yards to the base of the hill. Then, leave the Woodward Valley Trail and walk 60-70 yards over the grassy slope to the top. When coming up from the Coast Trail follow the Woodward Valley Trail to a point where it levels off and turns southwest (about 1/2 mile from Coast Trail junction). Stop, turn around and observe the hill 50 yards in front of you.

A view south towards Driftwood Beach and McClures Beach

Wildcat Camp and Beach as seen from above on the Coast Trail

Wildcat Beach and Camp
A Magic Moment

"We sat down, in silence, for what must have been a half hour, each person absorbed in a particular facet of the mystical scene which the world around us had become."

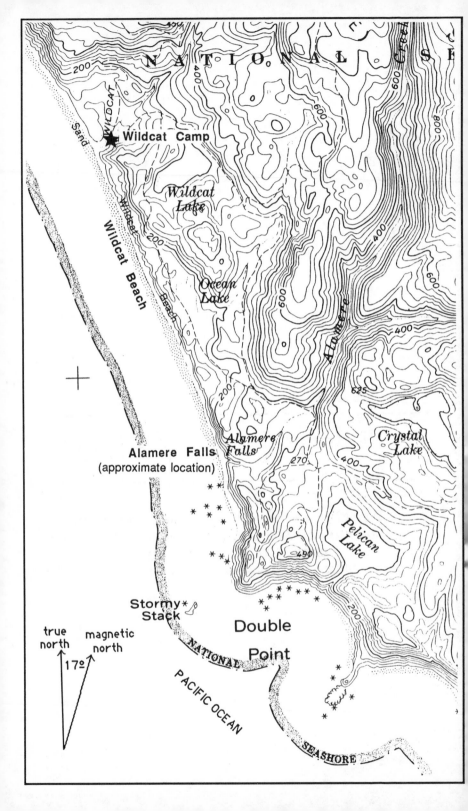

B eneath the full or near full moon Wildcat Camp,[1] situated in an open meadow 200 yards from Wildcat Beach, is an experience in serenity and reverence. Two nights before it is full, the moon will be high enough to illuminate the camp and beach as the afterglow of sunset fades into the night.

Sitting on the bluff at the western end of the camp and looking out to sea one October evening, I watched the sun in deepening colors of yellow, orange and crimson. The air was still, as is more the case in fall than in spring and summer, and, thus, the sea was nearly placid. Only one line of almost miniature breakers gently turning over and the occasional far off screeching of a gull somewhere down the beach broke the hush of evening.As the sea pulled at the sun and the huge orange-crimson ball began approaching the horizon a thin veil of cold mist began slowly forming along the beach rendering the breakers less distinct. In this compelling scene I found myself becoming strangely absorbed. I was not aware of any particular object nor did my eyes search the scene. Instead, I became transfixed as though day dreaming. The world, including, myself had become one massive kaleidoscope of magenta and crimson. Then, gradually, the sun slipped behind the horizon leaving behind its hues of magenta and maroon across the western sky. Suddenly a squadron of some ten or twelve pelicans, flying in line and in silhouette against the sky some 400 yards out to sea, brought me back to the buff. Almost instinctively, I turned to look over my shoulder and there, just over the Olema Ridge to the east,

---

[1] Wildcat Camp is approximately 6 hiking miles from the three closest traiheads – Palomarin, Fire Brooks, and Bear Valley. Approaching from Five Brooks and Bear Valley involves close to 1000 feet of up and downhill hiking. The approach from Palomarin is much more level. Overnight camping at Wildcat Camp requires prior

hovered a brilliant yellow near full moon. It was too low and the afterglow of sunset too strong to allow much illumination but, turning back to the sea, I noticed the reflection of the moon already flashing on the underbellies of churning breakers.

Southern Wildcat Beach and Double Point.

Gradually the flashing became brighter and the line of whitecap along the extended crest of breakers became whiter as the twilight faded to moonlight. The tide was receding and, as it did so, it left a long band of wet sand as evidenced by the reflective illumination given it by the rising moon.

The air was now colder and, feeling a need for my down jacket, I sauntered back across Wildcat Meadow to my campsite. Clusters of other campers huddled around their low burning charcoal fireplaces. The meadow was now well lighted by the moon, and I could make out the various colors of the jackets worn by the campers and the colors of tents scattered across the meadow. The noisy chatter that one sometimes hears in mid afternoon at Wildcat Camp had faded to barely audible murmurs. I noticed that a few individuals, sitting in silence on table tops, seemed to be gazing across the landscape as though their attention and quiet had been commanded by the beauty.

I decided to go out to the beach and walk to Alamere Falls, a place which I had seen many times by daylight but had never seen in moonlight. A few of my companions decided to join me and in a few minutes we were gliding on wet hard packed sand towards a distant waterfall one mile down the beach. While we could see the silhouette of cliffs and hills above the beach, we could not yet see the waterfall which plunges over a 35 foot cliff onto the sands of Wildcat beach. The light of the moon on the wet sand of the low tide moved just ahead of us, flashing brilliantly and, in places, reflecting a discernible image of the moon. As we moved along in the moonlight, faces clearly visible, the muffled sound of the still gentle breakers was ever constant. The subdued sea was harmonious with the gentleness of the landscape. Then, through the faint veil of mist, someone spotted Alamere Falls, a white ribbon which seemed detached from cliff and beach alike as it dangled in space. As we drew closer, and the falls became more distinct, the slapping sound of falling water gradually became audible above the incessant sound of churning breakers. Moon spangles danced in the small stream that ran from the base of the falls some 30 to 40 yards into the surf, the last of Alamere Creek before it became lost forever in the sea. We sat down, in silence, for what must have been a half hour, each person absorbed in a particular facet of the mystical scene which the world around us had become.

Back in camp an hour or so later, we disdained to crawl into our tents, long since set up, in order to sleep in the open and beneath the moon – morning frost be damned. Snuggled together in a row of five down cocoons, I remembered an experience which my life-long friend, Will Lotter, had had at Wildcat Camp a few years before and so I told the story as Will had related it to me.

Will and two of his sons were camped, one March, beneath the full moon at Wildcat Camp. Just as we were sleeping in the open rather than in tents in order to enjoy the moonlit landscape so had they. Around 2 am Will was awakened by, as he describes it, a "clacking" sound. He surveyed the moon drenched meadow and discovered, some 50 yards away, two white stags (Fallow deer) engaged in battle, locking horns and each trying to drive the other backwards. A semicircle of other white deer, mostly does and fawns, were watching the drama from a safe distance. Will awakened his two sons and, he said, the three of them watched the battle for perhaps a half hour when suddenly the struggle ended and the deer, stags included, slipped away up the hillside overlooking Wildcat Camp. When my story was concluded we searched the meadow and surrounding hillsides, chins propped up on forearms, for Fallow deer before giving up one by one to crawl deep inside sleeping bags in the enveloping cold.

Off and on during the night we awakened to gaze out across the silent and serene landscape. By early morning the air was crisp and dew was forming on the grass and, of course, on the sleeping bags. But amid such beauty no one abandoned the meadow for the tents. Around 3 am the moon was now low on the western horizon, moving towards the top of the bluff to the west. Shortly afterwards I awakened again to discover that the moon was lost from sight though the high hills to the east were still basking in soft moonglow. Realizing that the moon, which had slipped below the edge of the bluff, was within a few minutes of setting, I threw on a jacket, wiggled out of my sleeping bag, jumped into pants and shoes, and dashed to the edge of the bluff as some of the others followed after me. Just in time – the moon was barely above the horizon, deep yellow with a hint of orange. We sat in reverent silence until gradually the moon sank into the

Sunset along the beach

sea leaving behind a canopy of stars, especially to the east, in a sky darkened by the disappearance of the moon nearly two hours before the morning twilight. In darkness, then, we carefully picked our way across the landscape to catch a few more hours of sleep before the dawn brought another day to Wildcat Beach.

Dying whale at beach below Arch Rock Overlook

Whale Watching
A Magic Moment

"Watching a 30 to 40 ton, 40 to 50 foot, highly intelligent marine mammal in the middle of a 6000 to 8000 mile migration is an awe inspiring experience."

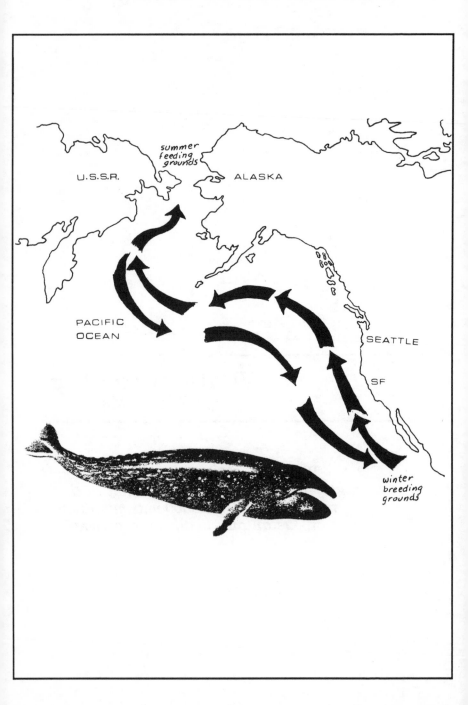

I am not a naturalist by formal training or self-education. I am primarily an explorer and, especially a nature lover. My powerful affinity for the beauty of nature is in no way increased by what I do happen to know about the life cycle and habits of flora and fauna. My sense of wonder and reverence in the presence of a landscape is not, for example, enhanced by my knowledge of the deer grazing or the flowers growing upon it. However, the study of natural history is as legitimate as the appreciation of natural surroundings, so it is in that recognition that I approach much of the content of this chapter on whale watching at Point Reyes National Seashore. I have relied in this chapter on research and interrogation of those knowledgeable [1] about whales.

Off the Point Reyes coast - as off coastal regions of the rest of California - various types of marine mammals, including whales, travel either because the California coast, or Point Reyes in particular, is their habitat or because they are migrating from one region to another. Many different kinds of whales may be seen off the California coast, but the best known and most frequently seen is the gray whale.

Gray whales average 35 to 40 feet in length at maturity. They weigh between 20 and 40 tons! Gray whales are "baleen" in that instead of teeth they have hundreds of fringed plates hanging from their upper jaws to act as a kind of sieve. The baleen sieve filters plankton, small schooling fish, and other forms of small sea life. Thus, the gray whale is a kind of grazer unlike toothed whales which are predators searching the sea for larger fish which they sieze and then crush with their teeth.

---

[1] I am particularly indebted to Bill Randolph of the Terwilliger Nature Education Center in Corte Madera, CA.

As with other baleen whales, the female gray is slightly larger than the male. The female gives birth in warm waters of Baja California, Mexico to a calf roughly 15 feet long and 1500 pounds in weight. The life span of gray whales is usually 30 to 40 years though some may live as long as 60 years. A distinguishing feature of gray whales is the absence of a dorsal fin, that rudder-like object that protrudes from the back of many other types of whales. The gray whale   is, of course, gray in color though it may have a mottled appearance due to the presence of barnacles[2] and orange colored "whale lice" attached to its skin. The gray whale, along with other baleen whales, has two blow holes above its snout, whereas toothed whales (dolphins and porpoise) have one.

The pregnant females leave the Bering Sea off Alaska in October after having spent the summer with males, non pregnant females and juveniles feeding in the waters of Alaska.[3] The migrating female, now at late term pregnancy (the gestation period is 11 1/2 to twelve months) travels southward 6000 to 8000 miles at a rate of 2 to 4 knots (top speed is 10 knots) for 15 to 20 hours a day until reaching the warm waters of Baja California, Mexico. Here she will give birth to her calf. [4] Although sometimes calves are born *during* the southward migration. Birth during migration increases the chance of death by predators (orcas or great whites) or from hyperthermia. Thus, the journey from Alaska to Baja California takes 2 1/2 to 3 months, from October to sometime

---

[2] A gray whale may eventually carry around as much as 1000 pounds of barnacles.

[3] The whales feed on crustaceans located on the sandy bottom of the Bering Sea.

[4] A mother provides up to 50 gallons of milk a day for her calf. The calf may gain up to 65 pounds a day in the first few weeks of its life.

in December. Following the pregnant females by a few weeks are the males, non-pregnant females and juveniles. Whereas the pregnant females travel in groups of two or three, or alone, the second group swims in groups of up to 12, taking six to eight weeks to reach Baja.

The return to Alaska is again characterized by two distinct migrations. The males, the newly impregnated females (who will, with a twelve month gestation period, return to Baja to give birth to their calves about 11 1/2 months later), and the juveniles leave Baja in February. By June they reach the Bering Sea. The mothers and calves remain behind in the warm Baja waters for another month or more before beginning their northward migration in March. The calves need that extra month to develop a protective layer of blubber against the cold water. Mother and calf reach the Bering Sea in July.

During the migration from Alaska to Baja California, Mexico the gray whales of both migrating groups travel fairly close to shore - generally along the 300 foot contour line (ocean depth outer continental self or 300 feet off shore). This means that off Point Reyes itself the whales may be as close as two or three miles off-shore and thus visible from this vantage point which is 600 feet above sea level. On the northward migration mothers and calves travel much closer to shore, sometimes only a few hundred yards off the coastline, where, it is believed, the calves may be weaned and taught to eat solid food. It is, then, *in late March and April and May that gray whales - mothers and calves - come closest to shore affording the best opportunity for whale watching.*

At Point Reyes National Seashore the best location for whale watching is Point Reyes itself - to where one may drive on Sir

Francis Drake Boulevard, which begins at Greenbrae in Marin County (take the San Anselmo turn-off when traveling north on Highway 101 from San Francisco). During the northern migration other locations such as Panoramic Hill (see chapter bearing this name) will provide a commanding view of Drakes Bay and, thus, afford a good opportunity to see a mother and calf traveling close to shore.

The migrating gray whale will "blow" (exhale) up to l5 feet, and this may be the first indication that a whale may be in view. Since gray whales have two blow holes, the resulting blow is somewhat heart-shaped, though this may not be discernible when the wind is whipping the surf into whitecaps. The gray whale will blow three to five times with 30 to 60 seconds between each blow before it dives below the surface again. A gray whale will blow once for about each 60 seconds it spends under water. On a calm and sunny day you may see the reflection of the sun on the shiny wet back of the whale. However, on on overcast days there is less glare and, thus, a better opportunity for sighting a whale. The whales may reveal themselves by breeching (leaping out of the water, turning onto their backs, and plunging back with an enormous splash). [5] Grays may breech two or three times in a row. Breeching may have something to do with courtship, dislodgeing barnacles and parasites or, in the case of calves, exercise or frolic.

Whales will sound (deep dive, almost straight down), flipping preliminary to the sound and, thus, showing, briefly, their butterfly-shaped tail. They may also engage in "skyhopping" - a position in which the whale floats vertically in the water with its head eight

---

[5] Gray whales are the second most common breeching whale.

to ten feet above the surface. In this action the whale is probably getting its bearings or checking out such obstructions as nearby boats.

Binoculars are a must for the whale watcher, but spot the whale first with the naked eye, then focus your binoculars. A powerful telephoto lens is a must for the photographer - 800 to 2000 mm. Warm clothing is also a must. You would do well to call the Visitor Center in advance for a weather and whale activity report. At Point Reyes the vantage point is often shrouded in fog or beset by strong winds even on clear days. A clear day in December or January is sometimes ideal to view the southward migrating whale - warm, windless, and with excellent visibility. One can expect less glare in the morning hours. Watching a 30 to 40 ton, 40 to 50 foot, highly intelligent marine mammal in the middle of a 6000 to 8000 mile migration is an awe inspiring experience.

VANTAGE POINTS for whale watching at Point Reyes National Seashore:

• Point Reyes itself. The most commanding view is near the Point Reyes Lighthouse.

• On the Coast Trail some 300-600 vertical feet above Miller Point. An excellent view of Drakes Bay.

• On the Woodward Valley Trail, at the point where the trail breaks out into the open at 500 feet above sea level. Face the ocean, then look 45 degrees to your right to a small nearby hill some 50 feet higher than where you are standing. Walk 100 yards to the top of this hill. See the chapter, Panoramic Hill).

• Along the Coast Trail above WIldcat Camp there is a spot amid pine trees, near old boarded up forts. Immediately south of the pine trees, there is a dramatic view of Drakes Bay.

• Along the Coast Trail, in the first two miles north of Palomarin Trailhead, there are places with a good view of the ocean.

• Along the Coast Trail between Coast Camp and a point where it turns inland towards the Hostel there are a number of locations just west of the trail where one can have a good view of Drakes Bay.

• Near Kelham Beach, at the promontory of Point Resistance, above Secret Beach, and above Sculptured Beach.

•The hills along the Limantour Road as the road crests and begins to drop towards Limantour parking lot, is especially good in April and May.

For current information on whale watching at Point Reyes National Seashore conducted by the National Park Service or by private organizations call the Point Reyes Visitor Center {415) 663-1092.

More information about whales and whale migrations is available from the following organizations in California:

•Greenpeace, San Francisco (415) 474-6767

•Oceanic Society, San Francisco (415) 441-1104

•Lawrence Hall of Science, Berkeley (415) 642-5132

•The American Cetacean Society, San Pedro (213) 548-6279

•Project Jonah, San Francisco (415) 205-9846

•Terwilliger Nature Education Center,
  Corte Madera (415) 927-1620

Grasses along the Point Reyes hills

A Walk in the Piny Woods
A Magic Moment

"...one is compelled to sit down amid the pine trees, with their almost overpowering aroma, and surrender, for a momemnt, to nature. And to know, again, what it is to be truly rich."

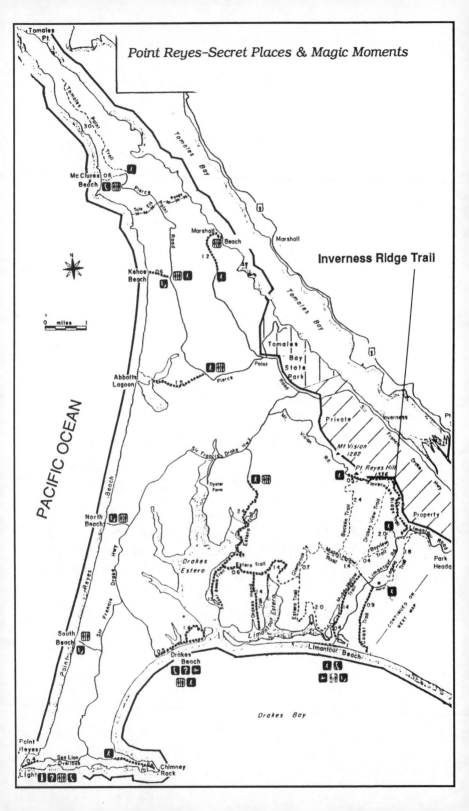

Point Reyes–Secret Places & Magic Moments

Inverness Ridge Trail

O n a warm spring day in April or May, preferably on a weekday, drive to the Bayview Trailhead on the Limantour Road and take an easy walk through the *piny woods* (Bishop pines) on the Inverness Ridge Trail to Point Reyes Hill (1336'). Readers with roots in the piny woods of the deep south, those who are homesick for the sub alpine belt of the Sierra Nevada Summer, or anyone who loves the aroma of a pine forest on a warm spring or summer day will find this walk a nostalgic experience.

The first .7 mile along the Inverness Ridge Trail from the Bayview Trailhead is characterized by a generally broad road-trail affording panoramic westward views of the northern fringe of Drakes Bay as contained by the long arm of Point Reyes itself. On the east side the trail is paralleled by a thick forest of Bishop pines with their rugged bark, cones extending all along the branches, and flat crowns. After .7 mile the road-trail changes to a conventional trail-path[1] and the thick piny woods begin – the thickest section of Bishop pines at Point Reyes National Seashore. The warm sweet aroma is powerfully nostalgic for anyone who has lived or roamed piny woods anywhere. In places the trail is covered with crunchy pine needles. Fallen branches and cones lie scattered along, and sometimes across, the trail. The forest is thick – tree trunks of 6-15 inches in circumference standing 3 to 5 feet apart while the highest crowns reach to 50 feet or more above the forest floor. Shrubs of all descriptions crush in on the trial from both sides – coyote brush, huckleberry, California lilac, deer brush, blackberry, thimbleberry, and

---

[1] At .7 mile the Inverness Ridge Trail comes upon a paved road, off of which two driveways lead to secluded residences. The trail has brushed the western fringe of Inverness. Standing on the paved road, which turns upward into the forest, look to the left, some 50 yards from a Park Service gate behind you, and you will find the Inverness Ridge Trail traversing the western slope of the forested hillside. As of this writing no trail sign is posted to help the hiker out of a confusing situation.

manzanita. I was surprised to see, one March, yellow monkey flower, which grows in wet places, sprouting up only 25 feet from orange monkey flower which grows only in dry places. And, in spring, the forget-me-nots, at ankle and shin high level, cheer those hiking along. Here, in the Bishop pine forest on a warm day, the mood is intimate. Drakes Bay to the west is almost entirely lost from view for the next mile or more until one emerges, suddenly, from the forest at an open meadow with a fine view of Tomales Bay to the northeast.

The terrain is now as open as it had been enclosed. The view towards Tomales Bay, 1 1/2 miles away, is characterized by a thick pine forest sweeping from below the meadow almost to the shore of Tomales Bay. The pine forest, with its flat crowns, looks somewhat like a tropical rain forest.

From the open meadow the trail, situated now at the base of Point Reyes Hill, 330 feet above and 1/2 mile beyond, moves upward on the southeast flank of the hill (at 1336'). In half a mile one catches sight of the fence setting off a navigational facility atop Point Reyes Hill. At this point one can break off the main trail, which heads for the dirt road on the summit just past the east side of the navigational facility, and follow a footpath 150 yards to an open meadow slanting westward. Here a climax panorama spreads from the southern end of Limantour Beach to Abbotts Lagoon – 5 to 6 miles of rolling brush covered hills, wooded ravines, a thin line of sandy beach, a shimmering Drakes Bay, and long arms of Drakes and Limantour esteros extending inland from out of the bay. In the warm sun of a balmy spring afternoon the green hills glisten ever brightly. Paint brush, iris, poppies, and bush lupine break the consistency of green hillside.

Though the return route is the same as the approach it is a direction opposite to that of the approach. The sun, having traveled father on its westward path, casts longer and different shadows. Meadows which were lighted in the morning are now in soft shade. Others which were without the morning sun now bask in the light of the late afternoon. The pine tops gently sway and softly sing in the afternoon breeze. Poppies which have lost the afternoon sun have begun to close up. And one is compelled to sit down amid the pine trees, with their almost overpowering aroma, and surrender, for a moment, to nature. And to know, again, what it is to be truly rich.

Moonset along Point Reyes hills

On the threshold of Divide Meadow – Bear Valley Trail

Bear Valley by moonlight
A Magic Moment

*"Under the light of a full, or nearly full, moon
Bear Valley becomes intriguing, somewhat
haunting, and, yet gentle and comforting."*

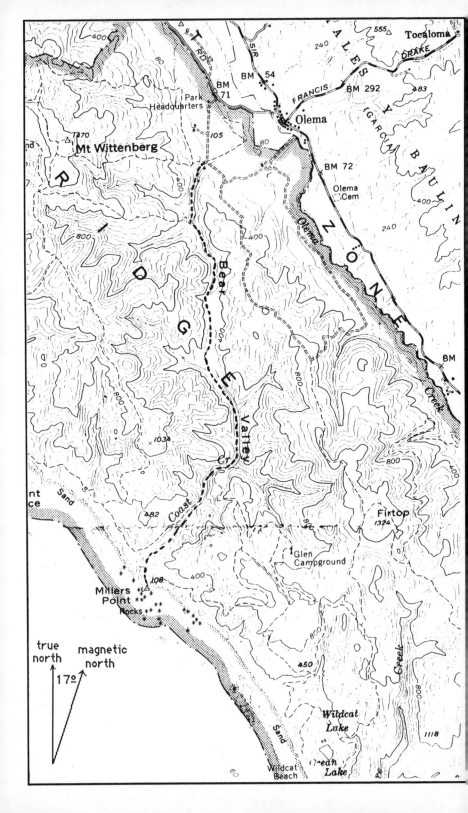

Bear Valley, in Point Reyes National Seashore, is 4.2 miles long. It extends from the Visitor Center near Olema to where it reaches the sea at Arch Rock Overlook. The valley is really two valleys divided by a low section in the Olema Ridge at Divide Meadow[1] 1.6 miles from Bear Valley Trailhead[2]. The trail, running the length of the valleys, is probably the most popular trail in the National Seashore. In virtually every season of the year on a Saturday or Sunday some 300 hikers cover the 4.2 miles of Bear Valley in one direction or the other. The protective arms of mother nature, in the form of bay trees arching over the trail through much of its length, give Bear Valley a maternal feeling. A stately original stand of Douglas firs tower 75-100 feet upward, erect and proud, guarding the valley at their feet. Sword ferns, thimbleberry, hazelnut, gooseberry, deer brush, alders, nettle, buckeye trees, and groves of forget-me-nots (in the spring), and other low lying vegetation crush in on the trail from out of the dense forests on either side. This consistency is broken by a large meadow, Divide Meadow, 1.6 miles from Bear Valley Trailhead. The main meadow, sloping 5-8 degrees to the west, is nearly 350 yards long. It constitutes the last resting place for hikers returning from the interior of the Seashore to Bear Valley Trailhead or a fine family picnic setting on a sunny day in any season of the year. At twilight deer can sometimes be seen grazing on the far fringes of the meadow. Occasionally a red tailed hawk swoops over the meadow as it moves to a tree top perch on the edge of the forest. Bear Valley has its aromas too –

---

[1] Divide Meadow is so named because all the streams east of the meadow run eastward into Tomales Bay, while all the streams west of the meadow flow westward to Drakes Bay.

[2] Bear Valley Trailhead and the Visitor Center are located in the same place and may be considered one and the same.

warm and pungent in the summer – cold and indescribably different in winter when very little sun gets through the tall firs on the south side.All this, and more, is well known to the thousands of hikers and cyclists who have traveled through Bear Valley over the 25 plus years the Seashore has been in existence. Very few of these travelers, however, have experienced the beauty of Bear Valley transformed by moonlight. At night, even a moonlit night, the valley is deserted as it is populated by day.

Under the light of a full, or nearly full, moon[3] Bear Valley becomes intriguing, somewhat haunting, and, yet, gentle and comforting. The trees of the surrounding forests are less distinct. All seem to blend together in a vague yellowish-green mass. Yet the shadows they cast are almost as distinct as shadows cast by daylight. Moon spangles dance softly to the gentle murmur of Coast Creek as it glides towards the sea. At Divide Meadow one can sometimes make out the vague forms of black tail deer or the ghost like focus of white (Fallow) deer grazing on the pale yellow grass. On a windless night, which is the rule in Bear Valley, a penetrating silence pervades the valley and there is a tendency to speak and walk softly rather than intrude on the quietness. One may even have the sense that there are no more people in the world and that one now has the world to oneself. Or that one is exploring a benign environment of some unknown planet on the outer reaches of the solar system. Faces are clearly seen at speaking distances in the full flood of moonlight. Even colors can be discerned at close range.

---

[3] The illumination of the moon is greatest from 3 days before the full moon to 3 days afterwards. However, 3 days before the moon rises full, it will already be high up in the sky when darkness befalls Bear Valley. This will likewise be the case 2 days before the full moon. On the night of the full moon one will need to wait 1 to 2 hours to give the moon time to rise high enough to illuminate the valley.

One can plan a moonlight outing in Bear Valley as part of a more comprehensive trip which would include traveling on to Wildcat Camp or Coast Camp for an overnighter. Or if stopping off at Wildcat Beach Overlook en route to Wildcat or Glen Camp. All these more encompassing trips provide unique aesthetic experiences. However, the experience of moonlight in Bear Valley is so especially unique as to recommend a journey to this place alone. Bear Valley by moonlight is best appreciated if the pace is unhurried, thus rendering the hiker more receptive to this unique aesthetic experience.

Meadow at Bear Valley Trailhead

A tidy tip

Kehoe Beach in May
A Magic Moment

"Few people know of the glorious scene that nature presents here each year in late spring."

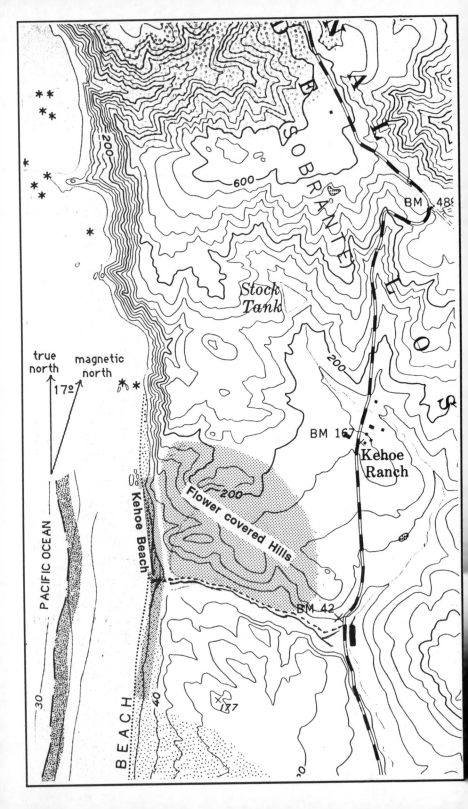

O ne of the most magnificent displays of single species of wild flowers at Point Reyes National Seashore takes place in May, in a year of average or better than average rainfall, on the sweeping hillsides north of Kehoe Beach. Few people know of the glorious scene that nature presents here each year in late spring. On a warm May weekend there may be 100 people on Kehoe Beach, but they never seem to stray from the .6 mile path taking them from the parking area to the beach. I've never seen more than 2 or 3 people on the surrounding hillsides which become, in May, a maze of yellow-white flowers.

Kehoe Beach, located in the extreme northern portion of Point Reyes National Seashore is 13 miles north of the National Seashore Headquarters in Olema by way of paved roadway. One must follow Francis Drake Blvd. to its junction with Pierce Ranch Rd., 7.3 miles from Park Headquarters/Visitor Center, then follow Pierce Ranch Road 5.6 miles to Kehoe Beach where one must park on a broad shoulder off the road.

The walk to Kehoe Beach is a level .6 mile. The path moves west through a low point in the hills running from Abbotts Lagoon to Tomales Bluff. To the left of the pathway a creek and marsh parallel the trail to the beach. To the right of the pathway the low lying hills roll gently upwards towards the high, and unseen, hill (534 feet) .5 mile east of Elephant Rock. Almost as soon as one begins walking on the beach access pathway tidy-tips will be seen splashed far and wide across the green hills to the right of the pathway. The hills to the left, across the marsh, are mostly brush covered and without many flowers other than a thick concentration of blue brush lupine, the thickest I've ever seen at Point Reyes.

To the right, or north, of the Kehoe Beach access trail the hills are ablaze with wild flowers – golden poppies, tidy tips, buttercups, dandelions, blue-eyed grass, iris still in evidence after an initial February bloom, and the magnificent yellow bush lupine with an aroma which permeates the air.[1] In a year of average or better than average rainfall the hills will be so thickly covered that one will need to exercise caution in walking or even sitting so as not to crush the flowers. On a sunny day the mostly yellow and golden flowers are incredibly radiant. This inspirational display spreads up and over the hills north of the Kehoe Beach Trail for a solid mile. A carpet of green and yellow-gold beneath a deep blue sky and with the distant crash of breakers for accompanying music. To the west an ocean of sun spangles dance merrily, as do the flowers, when the afternoon westerlies set a lively tempo in this beautiful natural theater under a sun very close to the summer solstice. All this within 50 miles of downtown San Francisco which seems, in such surroundings, nonexistent!

There is no set route one needs to take from the beach access pathway to the hills. I usually walk along the trail about 300 yards to the base of a small draw then climb on a cow path for some 400 yards to a small plateau with a fine view and then wander westward from there.

I have found the experience of wild flowers at Kehoe Beach most intense when by myself. So, if walking with friends try to split up for a half hour or more to see if you, too, find a solo with the flowers a heightened experience.

---

[1] For more information see *Flowers of Point Reyes National Seashore* by Roxanna S. Ferris.

View from Kehoe Beach to Point Reyes Beach

Passing through the sea tunnel under safe conditions

The Sea Tunnel in a storm
A Magic Moment

"The sound of the spectacle is as impressive as the sight. First there is the steady rumble of Coast Creek cascading down the last of its rocky course to the tunnel. In the background is the heavy to and fro swishing sound of ocean on the sea side of the tunnel, a side which one cannot see. Then comes a rumble, a whoosh, and the explosive roar as a wall of white water shoots through the tunnel and onto everything in its path."

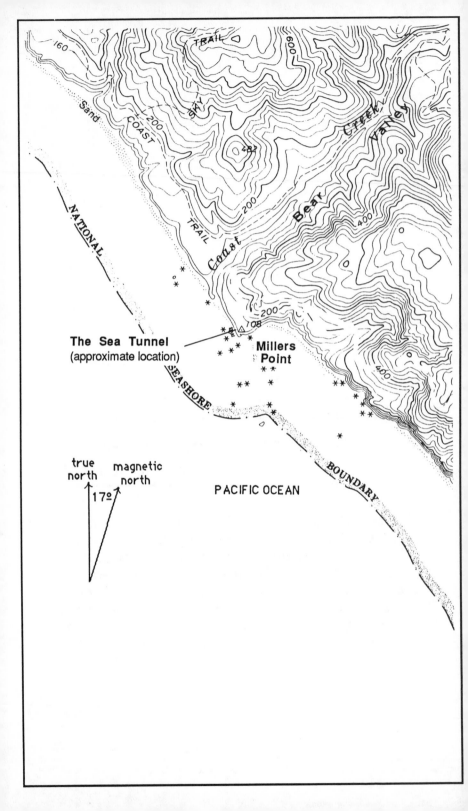

E veryone who has hiked in the Point Reyes hinterland knows the *Sea Tunnel* [1]. After having generally meandered, with an occasional fast run, for almost 3 miles Coast Creek, rising in the springs west of Divide Meadow, makes a sudden dash for the sea in a final 25 foot drop over some 75 yards of stream bed. At the end of this spurt Coast Creek, now in a deep ravine, comes pouring through the Sea Tunnel and out onto the narrow beach below the cliff of Arch Rock Overlook. Scores of people pass through the sea tunnel, wading, or jumping to keep their feet dry, every weekend. Others, more cautious, follow the access trail down from Arch Rock Overlook above to where it ends 25 feet from the tunnel. Here they perch themselves to watch the fun – high tide breakers merging with the stream water as it churns trash through the tunnel and hikers passing through while trying to stay dry.

The Sea Tunnel, however, is not known to many people during one of its most dramatic moments – when a heavy Pacific storm comes slamming into Drakes Bay and the Sea Tunnel in particular. This occasion is one of the most dramatic magic moments at Point Reyes National Seashore!

To witness this most unique drama one must be wearing clothing (wool and/or polypropylene) under 100% waterproof rain gear so that one will remain warm in windy wet weather. Even waterproof mittens or gloves are a good idea. Rather than a hat wear a wool

---

[1] Until the spring of 1986 there was a single tunnel, which my grandmother saw back in 1940 and which, no doubt, had been in existence at least 100 years before that. One weekend in April of 1986 I passed through the single tunnel and up along Coast Creek to Arch Rock Overlook as I must have 50 times before. On the very next weekend, after a week of heavy rain, a second tunnel appeared. The sea on one side and the stream on the other had done the inevitable almost before our very eyes.

cap under a rain jacket with a hood which can be tied under the chin. Waterproof boots with lug soles are important. And wool socks. Pack a big lunch with a thermos of a hot drink or soup. Then go for it – 4.2 miles straight down Bear Valley to Arch Rock Overlook to experience mother nature's spectacular at the Sea Tunnel.

First check the sea from the cliff over the beach to get some idea of tide conditions. Then move down the access trail, on the ravine side of Arch Rock Overlook, to a point where you can watch the spectacle safely. Proceed slowly so you can get an idea of how great the reach of the breakers is and, therefore, determine where a safe vantage point will be from either the far end of the trail or from the other side of the Coast Creek. The rocks will be slippery, but with proper soles and good judgement there should be no problem.

The sea will blast through the Sea Tunnel sending a thousand spears of white water crashing onto the rock wall opposite the tunnel, and onto the sands of the small beach immediately south of the stream as it makes a last turn before heading through the Sea Tunnel. The sea water will then race back through the tunnel as though being sucked through a stone straw (now two straws) by the unseen ocean on the other side of the tunnel. In its last 16 feet of run the stream virtually disappears for 10 to 15 seconds under the huge mass of seawater first blasting in and then rushing headlong back to the sea in the opposite direction.

The sound of the spectacle is as impressive as the sight. First there is the steady rumble of Coast Creek cascading down the last of its rocky course to the tunnel. In the background is the heavy to and fro swishing sound of ocean on the sea side of the tunnel, a side which one cannot see. Then comes a rumble, a whoosh, and the explosive roar as a wall of white water shoots through the tunnel and onto everything in its path.

Needless to say one should not attempt to pass through the Sea Tunnel under these conditions. The sight of the very first blast of the sea through the Sea Tunnel should make this word of caution something of an understatement.

Heavy seas and high tide at the sea tunnel

Moonrise over Drakes Bay as seen from viewpoint as described

Moonrise at Drakes Beach
A Magic Moment

"On a windless evening a hush falls across land and sea broken only by the muffled sound of the now tranquil surf and far-off screech of seagull far down the beach."

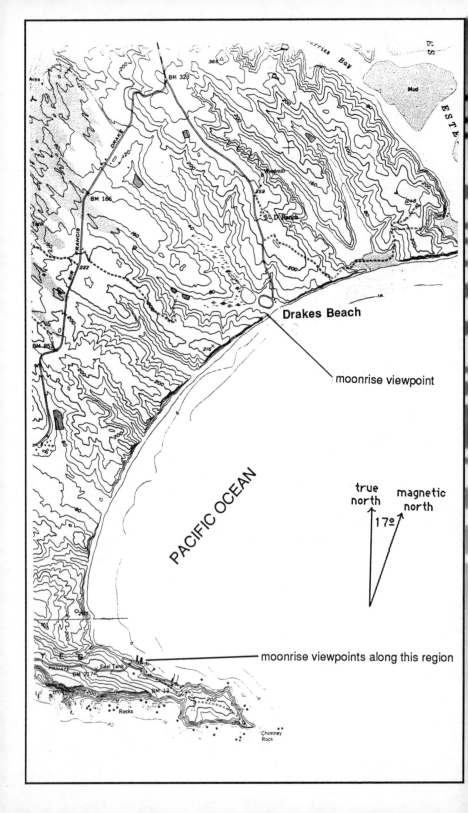

Drakes Beach

moonrise viewpoint

PACIFIC OCEAN

true north | magnetic north

17°

moonrise viewpoints along this region

Chimney Rock

This magic moment, unlike so many at Point Reyes National Seashore, involves a minimum of walking and should appeal to those who, for whatever reason, do not or are not able to walk appreciable distances. All that is necessary is to drive to the parking lot at the Kenneth C. Patrick Visitor Center at Drakes Beach. Then walk 75 yards from the parking lot to the beach or, preferably, 100 yards on a paved path to a prepared viewpoint on top of a buff, north of the parking lot, overlooking the sea.[1] Be in position, on the bluff, at least 15 minutes before the full moon rise having, of course, checked the weather in the newspaper but, also, at the Kenneth C. Patrick Visitor Center (open only week-ends, phone # [415] 669-1250) or the Bear Valley Visitor Center (phone#[415] 663-1092) to make sure local ocean fog has not or will not obscure the scene.

The moon will rise directly across Drakes Bay – above the Olema Ridge 4 miles or so above and beyond Limantour Spit and Beach. The full moon will appear somewhat enlarged, as it always does upon rising, due to the distorting effect of the earth's atmosphere. It will appear about 15 minutes after it is officially listed to rise because, from your Drakes Beach viewpoint, the moon must climb above the Olema Ridge. The sun will have slipped below the western horizon which, like the eastern horizon, is hidden from view by an intervening land mass, in this case Point Reyes itself. Since the full moon will, at Drakes Beach, follow the setting of the sun by a number of minutes the twilight will have faded sufficiently for the moon to cast quite a discernible shaft of light straight across Drakes Bay from shore to shore the minute it first appears. On a clear evening the sun's after glow to the west may cast a golden-orange hue all along the wet sand of the beach thus providing a magnificent display of

---

[1] Accessible to wheelchairs

deepening colors. On a windless evening a hush falls across land and sea broken only by the muffled sound of the now tranquil surf and the far-off screech of seagull far down the beach. The arc of cliffs, which may have been the ones reminding Sir Francis Drake of England's cliffs of Dover, pick up the reflected light of alpenglow from the sandy beach stretching at the foot of the cliffs. Sanderlings, in their eternal quest for food, sprint hither and yon behind the tide, oblivious to the incredible beauty engulfing the world around them.

This sublime moment will be equally or even more appreciated if one witnesses the spectacle from the small access road which turns westward off Sir Francis Drakes Boulevard, 1.25 miles from the parking lot at the Point Reyes Lighthouse. This road, 1.2 miles in length, runs towards, but not to, Chimney Rock on the eastern end of Point Reyes itself. From almost anywhere on the north slope hillsides facing Drakes Bay and Drakes Beach, or from the shoreline itself, one has a perfect vantage point for the moonrise. The view will include more of Drakes Bay and the high cliff above the bay than is the case from Kenneth C. Patrick Visitor Center at Drakes Beach a few miles north. The shaft of moonspangles cast by the just risen moon will be longer than the same shaft of light seen at Drakes Beach. One has a perfect view of the entire arc of beach and cliffs encompassing Drakes Bay from Point Reyes, where one now stands, to Double Point some 16 miles along the beach or 11 miles straight across the bay.

Photographers will find the moonrise at Drakes Beach a challenging and potentially rewarding experience. A tripod is of course, essential since shutter speeds will be very low for all but the very fastest films. And, long after the sun goes down on a most rare evening of broken clouds and rain squalls, the photographer may find the most elusive photographic subject the moon and the moon alone, can provide – a lunar rainbow.[2]

Two locations cited in this chapter provide very expansive panoramas thus increasing the chance of seeing a lunar rainbow when the exceedingly rare conditions exist.

To experience a miniature and *homemade* lunar rainbow so as, perhaps to whet one's appetite for such a spectacle in nature try the following: with the moon at 3/4 or greater, and after there is not trace of sunset alpengow, drag your garden hose into the front or backyard, whichever area is completely flooded in moonlight. Direct a fine and wide spray of water into the air at about a 45° angle and in a direction opposite to the moon. For your neighbors this puzzling and seemingly eccentric behavior may necessitate prior notice. Better yet, invite them to witness something they may wait a lifetime to see in nature. When I did this the hysterical laughter of neighbors faded into silence and awe. And *my* lunar rainbow was only miniature.

---

[2] Lunar rainbows, as the infinitely more common solar rainbows, appear in the opposite direction to the source of light. I have seen only one, outside of the waterfall spray in Yosemite Valley, in 47 years exploring the wilderness. And I've made an active search, when conditions were right, since I first saw one in the Minaret Wilderness of the Sierra Nevada in 1971. At Point Reyes, on any moonlit evening when the moon is from 3/4 to full and when broken clouds and occasional shower conditions exist you might see a lunar rainbow which, incidentally, is silver-white, not colored.

Sunrise from Mount Wittenberg

Mount Wittenberg
A Magic Moment

*"The Beauty of the moonlit world above
the sea of fog was too compelling to leave..."*

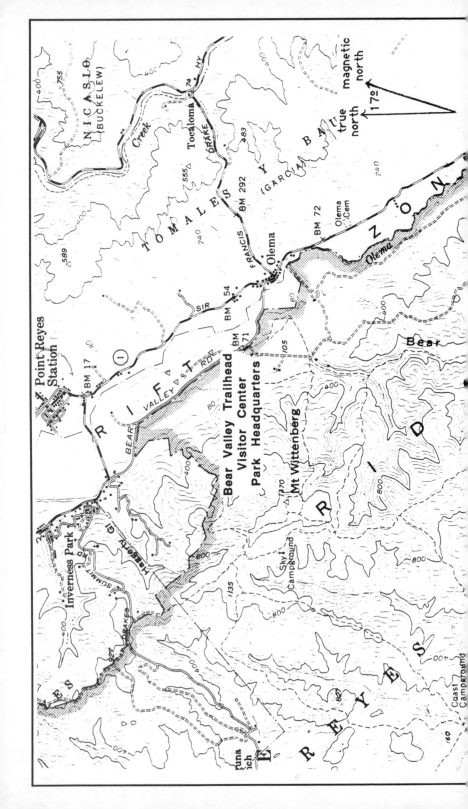

Mount Wittenberg is no secret place. Many a hiker scurries up the short summit access trail (approximately 300 yards and 200 vertical feet) to its generally open summit to enjoy the broad panoramas. Most of these hikers, who are most numerous on weekends, are unaware that there are certain natural circumstances which transform Mount Wittenberg into a profound mystical experience. These circumstances – or conditions– are infrequent. However, they can be anticipated with fair prospect that they will occur. The reward for the patience and perseverance necessary to discover these special conditions is a truly indelible experience.

One Sunday in February a number of years ago I had finished leading a college group on a day hike in Point Reyes National Seashore and had returned to my home in Redwood City about 9 pm. The night was clear with a full moon and, as I pulled into my driveway, I realized I should have stayed at Point Reyes after dismissing my hikers. So I grabbed my sleeping bag and drove straight back to the Bear Valley Trailhead where I arrived around 11 pm.

As I got out of the car in the crisp night air, I noticed that thin veils of ground fog were forming all around me in isolated pockets. Each pocket of fog was roughly 20-30 feet high and from 20-40 yards in length though the areas between pockets were misty and indistinct. The scene had an ethereal look in the light of the full moon now high in the heavens. Moving up the Sky Trail, without flashlight, I glided beneath the overhanging bay and fir branches of the dense forest that encloses much of the trail as it climbs towards the summit of Mount Wittenberg (1407 feet). As I moved briskly upward I found myself entering isolated pockets of fog, thin wisps actually, all lighted with a delightfully eerie moonglow. The night was still. Not a breath of air stirred. No other figure – animal or human – was seen as I moved on past occasional open meadows and from pocket to pocket of ethereal fog. Occasionally, I was compelled to stop and listen to the silence and allow myself to be absorbed in the moon drenched landscape.

Approaching the summit of Mount Wittenberg, I noticed that the still air seemed warmer and there were no more fog pockets in evidence. However, as I turned to look down the slope of Mount Wittenberg I noticed that the isolated fog pockets were merging and thickening to form a massive veil which stretched from the horizon to a point 300 feet below me. Faintly visible above the enveloping white sea was Black Mountain behind Point Reyes Station, Mount Tamalpais, and both the Bolinas and Olema Ridges. I sat on the summit transfixed for what must have been an hour. The beauty of the moonlit world above a sea of fog was too compelling to leave, so I returned to the summit, bundled myself in down pants and parka, and spent the night watching in reverence. Sometime around 4 a.m. or 5 a.m. I must have fallen asleep for suddenly the bright light of the rising sun awakened me to yet another profound experience – the sun coming up over distant Mount Diablo as it, and the handful of other peaks and high ridges of the Bay Area (Twin Peaks, Tamalpais, Diablo, Black Mountain, Mount Vision, and the Olema Ridge) floated above like so many islands in a mysterious white sea.

From the summit of Mount Wittenberg the moonset is a profound experience, a mystical moment in the life of any mortal willing to take the time to simply sit in silence and watch. Moonsets from the time of the waxing half moon to the full moon are the best simply because after the full moon sets successive moonsets take place in daylight and the glow of the moon is lost in the bright light of the day. The ideal lighting for a viewing is just before dawn on the day when the moon will rise full some 13-14 hours later. So if the moon is to be full on the night, say, of August 2 at 8 p.m. the best lighting for the moonset will be earlier that morning at about 5 a.m. August 2. Always consult your local newspaper to find the exact times for risings and settings and thus you can effectively plan to be in position 15-30 minutes beforehand.

The evening of the rising full moon is another magical moment on Mount Wittenberg. In fact, one can first watch the sun set over Drakes Bay to the west then, facing the east, watch the full moon come looming up, a massive red-orange ball magnified by the atmosphere of the earth, behind the Barnaby Ridge some 4-5 miles to the east. Since the full moon rises full just a few minutes after the sun has set and since the moon rises approximately 50 minutes later each night/day one night before the moon is full one can watch a near full moon slightly above the horizon as the sun sets. Again, consult your local paper for the exact times of the rising and setting sun and moon.

The most comfortable way to experience the magic moments described here is to plan to spend the appropriate night(s) at Sky Camp 350-400 feet and 3/4 mile below Mount Wittenberg to the west. The easiest approach to Sky Camp is from the Sky Trailhead off Limantour Road. The elevation rise is less than 300 feet and the distance is roughly 1.2 miles. From Bear Valley Trailhead to Sky Camp via the Sky Trail is approximately the same distance but a 1200 feet elevation rise is involved.

Moonset at McClures Beach

McClures Beach
A Magic Moment

"The world was now a deep orange – the sky, the beach, and even the cliffs behind me."

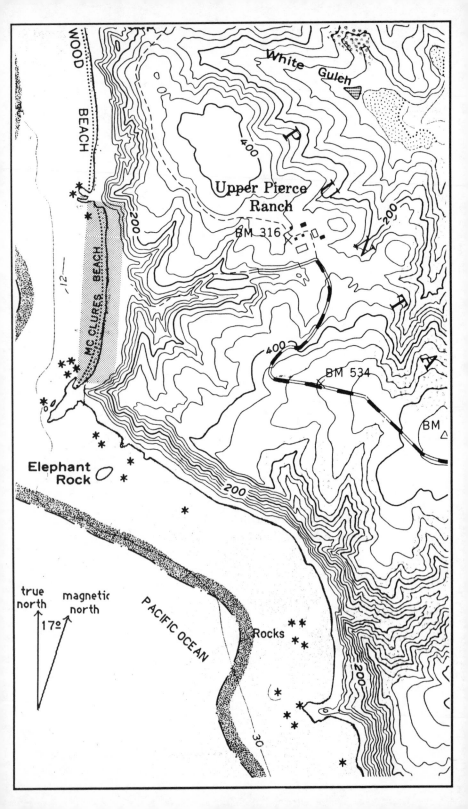

Mystical moments in time await those with the patience and determination to experience them at McClure Beach.

One warm late autumn afternoon I had been wandering around McClures Beach and Driftwood Beach, immediately north of McClures Beach, camera in hand. I had been trying so intently to capture seabirds in flight with a 500mm lens that I hadn't noticed the dramatic display of crashing breakers against the prominent seawall which jets out into the Pacific Ocean at the southern end of McClures Beach[1]. When I finally did take notice I was not moved to action because I already had photographed my share of dramatic seascapes at McClures Beach. Then, a few seconds later, a sudden rush of memory sent me jogging down the beach towards the seawall where my friend and wildlife photographer, Tom Rountree, had once gotten some unusual sunset pictures. So, I thought, why not see if I could do as well as Tom?

In three minutes I was in position – in line with the 10 feet of seawall, which encloses a small cove, and the sun resting 10 degrees above the rock and slowly sinking. In effect, I had my own rock wall horizon 75 yards away and with every 6th or 7th wave sending a magnificent spray of water skyrocketing above the wall and in front of the sun. As the sun slipped slowly lower, the western sky presented a deepening orange hue as background for the seawall. Then, though I could not see the wave on the ocean side of the seawall as it rolled forward I could hear the tremendous smacking sound created by the racing mass of water as it collided with the other side of the seawall. That

---

[1] This rock is sometimes confused with Elephant Rock which is slightly farther south and not seen from McClures Beach.

sound was my signal to quickly sight through my camera, now on tripod, and await what I hoped would be a colossal splash of water as it partially obscured the sun behind it. Because I was at a safe distance my camera and I remained dry.[2] I continued shooting for perhaps 10-12 minutes until the sun, still 20 minutes from setting, slipped behind the seawall. So I packed up, jogged up the beach and away from the seawall to get a line on the sunset, and began shooting anew. By this time the wet sand had taken on the orange hue of the western sky. Gradually the sun lost its intensity of light and I could look at it steadily with the naked eye as it now touched the sea. The world was now a deep orange – the sky, the beach, and even the cliffs behind me. In awe, I put the camera aside, sat down, and became totally absorbed in the scene. No picture can capture such beauty.

The experience of the setting sun at McClures Beach caused me to wonder if I could photograph the setting full moon under similar conditions – waves crashing above the seawall to partially obscure the moon. The problem, however, is there is only one day in each month when the lighting conditions are just right for such a photograph. That day, a moment actually, is roughly 30 minutes before the moonset in the morning twilight of the day when, some 15 hours later, the moon will rise full.[3] Further complicating the situation is the need for the right tide and surf conditions (medium to high tide with big breakers). And, of course, the weather must be good on the crucial day at the

---

2 The situation reminded me of a photography student who, anxious to be the first person to McClures Beach and, not knowing of the *9th wave* phenomenon at these particular rocks, raced to the lee side of the seawall. Needing to change film he quickly opened his camera and, totally absorbed in what he was doing, was oblivious to the ominous crash on the other side of the seawall. Seconds later he and his open camera were totally drenched. So hikers, as well as photographers, beware. You won't drown but there are many misfortunes short of that. At the very least, study the situation for a few minutes from a safe distance – conditions described do not always exist.

crucial moment. Seven different months over a 12 month period I tried without success usually because of fog or rain. Finally one April pre-dawn I discovered perfect weather, perfect tide, and totally placid sea.[4] However, I was pleased with the moonset pictures I got even if there were no dramatic sprays of seawater coming over the seawall. An all pervading bluishness spread across the land and the sea in the pre-dawn twilight. In sharp contrast, the moon cast a brilliant yellow light clear across the sea from the horizon to the wet sand at my feet. Only the faint sound of a single line of 10 inch breakers broke the total silence. And as the moon slipped slowly into the sea the blue of twilight gradually faded away while an orange glow along the eastern skyline above the cliffs told of the approach of another day at McClures Beach.

---

[3] The moon rises about 52 minutes later each day. The same is true of the moonset. The best lighting – enough twilight to make lengthy time exposures unnecessary – is just before the moonsets in the minutes before dawn on a day when it rises full in the evening. For example, If the moon is to rise full on August 1 at 7:30 pm the ideal moonset conditions, for the photographer, are in the half hour before the moonsets in the early morning, over 12 hours earlier, on August 1. Consult your local paper for the exact time of the moonset and be on the scene at least 30 minutes ahead of time.

[4] Once, with perfect conditions including ocean spray, I waited patiently for the moon to sink a little lower so as to nestle atop the seawall. Then, all of a sudden, the moon disappeared – in a distant fog bank I had not seen in the twilight!

ABOUT THE AUTHOR

Native Californian, Phil Arnot is an active and highly regarded mountaineer, explorer and photographer. He has explored extensively in the Olympic Mountains of Washington, the Cascade Mountains of Oregon and Washington, the High Sierra of Yosemite and Sequoia National Park, New Zealand and South America.

He has made numerous ascents, including Mt. Mckinley and hiked over 8000 trail and off-trail miles in the western wilderness.

He leads wilderness trips throughout the western United States, Alaska and Point Reyes National Seashore.

Coauthor of *Exploring Point Reyes, Run for Your Life, San Francisco—A City to Remember,* and author of *The Mystique of the Wilderness.*

other travel & travel related books from

Wide World Publishing/Tetra

P.O. Box 476 • San Carlos, CA 94070

HAWAII–*Island Paradise*

An artistic representation of the Hawaiian experience •. Illustrations are paired with quotations from Mark Twain, Jack London, Isabella Bird, John La Farge, Pegge Hopper and others. This book is a collection of impressions by a variety of visitors to the island paradise of Hawaii. Helps rekindle the memories of multihued skies, the fragrance of plumeria blossoms and the caresses of the tradewinds. Evokes the mood of aloha!

•156 pages•illustrations•81/2"x11"
•ISBN:0-9331742-42-X•$9.95

GREEK COOKING FOR EVERYONE
by Theoni Pappas & Elvira Monroe

The extensive and authentic recipes are arranged by menus for 22 complete dinners. This format helps take the guesswork out of deciding what to serve with what. Special sections on desserts, breads, wines, coffee, cheeses, herbs and delicacies from the vendors.

" Stirs Greek spirit and captures the essense of Greek cooking ... a good gift for non-Greek cooks as well as those who collect Greek recipes. —Hellenic Journal

• 167 pages with 66 B/Wphotos of Greece
•ISBN: 0-933174-29-2• $7.95

HAWAII–Cooking with Aloha
by Elvira Monroe & Irish Margah

This book will help recreate the wonder and moods of a vacation in Hawaii's tropical paradise. 130 recipes include countless pupus•main dishes ranging from Kalua pig to curries•side dishes such as Portugese bean soup, lomi salmon and baked bananas •salads•breads•beverages. Special desserts include Mai Tai Pie, Kona Coffee Ice Cream Pie, Macadamia Nut Pie, Papaya Chiffon and Pineapple cheesecakes. Menus for a luau, dinner, suppers, barbeques and brunches are an added feature. Further enchancing the book are hints on decor, information on various islands and guidelines on selecting papayas, avocadoes and pineapples. Relive the magic of the tradewinds, swaying palms, white sands and the blue sky and sea.

•199 pages with illustrations•Over 130 recipes•ISBN: 0-933174-22-5•$7.95

---

*Available from your local bookstore or directly from
Wide World Publishing/Tetra, postage prepaid.*